PIT BULLS

and
Tenacious
GUARD DOGS

TS-141

Title page: American Pit Bull Terrier owned by Charles M. Kopenhafer.

Distributed in the UNITED STATES by T.F.H. Publications, Inc., One T.F.H. Plaza, Neptune City, NJ 07753; in CANADA to the Pet Trade by H & L Pet Supplies Inc., 27 Kingston Crescent, Kitchener, Ontario N2B 2T6; Rolf C. Hagen Ltd., 3225 Sartelon Street, Montreal 382 Quebec; in CANADA to the Book Trade by Macmillan of Canada (A Division of Canada Publishing Corporation), 164 Commander Boulevard, Agincourt, Ontario M1S 3C7; in ENGLAND by T.F.H. Publications, PO Box 15, Waterlooville PO7 6BQ; in AUSTRALIA AND THE SOUTH PACIFIC by T.F.H. (Australia) Pty. Ltd., Box 149, Brookvale 2100 N.S.W., Australia; in NEW ZEALAND by Ross Haines & Son, Ltd., 82 D Elizabeth Knox Place, Panmure, Auckland, New Zealand; in the PHILIPPINES by Bio-Research, 5 Lippay Street, San Lorenzo Village, Makati, Rizal; in SOUTH AFRICA by Multipet Pty. Ltd., P.O. Box 35347, Northway, 4065, South Africa. Published by T.F.H. Publications, Inc. Manufactured in the United States of America by T.F.H. Publications, Inc.

PIT BULLS
and
Tenacious
GUARD DOGS

Dr. Carl Semencic

ACKNOWLEDGMENTS

Over the course of the many years that I have had an intense interest in purebred dogs, I have communicated and shared ideas with and been offered information by so many people that to acknowledge the hoard who deserve recognition here is well beyond me. For this I sincerely apologize. I thank the many of you throughout Europe, South America, the Orient and from every nook and cranny of the United States who helped me to indulge myself in one of my favorite pastimes, "talking dogs." Although I can't list everyone's name here, you know who you all are and so do I.

I would like to take this opportunity to make special mention of a few folks by name however. I'd like to recognize Eddie Dombish, a very capable dog trainer based in New York City with whom I have talked dogs for so many hours on end over the years. Eddie is the kind of guy who is always ready to focus all of his energy upon a discussion about virtually any breed the world has ever known.

I'd also like to thank Roe Chen of the Bronx in New York City, another real dog enthusiast, show person, trainer, and breeder, for her general support, and Tobin Jackson not only for putting forth the effort to find me rare photographs of rare dogs just before this book went to press but also for being the incredibly energetic supporter of the purebred fancy that he is. Without guys like Tobin, this would be much less of a sport for all of us.

I'd like to thank Steve and Wendy Norris, the Bordeaux Dogue breeders for just everything from information, photographs, general discussion and enthusiasm to Texas Longhorn Burgers which, it is said, are leaner than flounder.

And again, I'd like to thank the rest of you.

DEDICATION

**This book is dedicated to my sons
Alexander Semencic
and
Daniel Richard Semencic
and to my wife Barbara.
Ain't we got fun?**

CONTENTS

" . . . a man-stopper is a dog possessing both the temperament and physical ability to stop a human intruder by inflicting such serious bodily harm as to render further advance physically impossible."

When a German Shepherd is good, it can be as good a guard dog as there has ever been.

INTRODUCTION

In order to avoid any confusion, readers should understand at the outset of this book that it is intended to be encyclopedic in nature; as such, it makes no attempt to instruct anyone in dog training techniques. Many good books covering both general training and protection training of dogs have already been written and are currently available. Anyone who feels the need for advice in this area should consult these other books.

As a guard dog encyclopedia, the purpose of this book is to introduce readers to the many varieties of effective home and personal guardian breeds that the world of purebred canines has to offer. It has been the author's observation that the average person who decides to own a guardian-type dog is often at a loss for sound ideas concerning the choice of breed of the prospective puppy. As fine a dog as a well-bred Doberman Pinscher or German

"My master's bigger than your master." It is not uncommon for big, imposing dogs to act aggressively towards one another. These two black and tan Germans are among the world's most popular guard dogs. Photo by Maria DiBenedetto.

Shepherd Dog can be, it is my opinion that their disproportionately high levels of popularity among purebred fanciers are due to a general lack of knowledge about reasonable alternatives to selecting these breeds.

An example of this lack of public understanding struck me just the other day as I dropped in on a friend who owns and operates an attack-dog training school. To make a long story short, his facility was brimming over with trained adult Doberman Pinschers, Rottweilers, and German Shepherd Dogs, each of which carried the usual high price tag. As we chatted, the owner of the school casually asked me if I knew anyone who wanted a two-year-old, well-bred, intelligent, fully housebroken, socialized, and trained male Giant Schnauzer for *free*. I knew the dog and expressed my opinion that it was a good animal. "Why free?" I asked. In the trainer's opinion, it was the best dog he had in the place, but due to the breed's relative lack of popularity among people in the market for a guard dog, it was obvious that the animal would never sell.

This book is intended to do away with such unfortunate misunderstandings. Those who are in search of an effective guard dog have many breeds of various types to choose from and should not feel limited to selecting from but a few. In fact, as the appropriate breed

treatments will discuss, the overpopularity that some of the better known guardian breeds are experiencing often renders them among the poorest choices that the novice purebred enthusiast can make in his or her search for a family guard dog.

Selecting a purebred puppy should be an interesting experience. The various histories that gave rise to the purebreds of today, combined with the serious effort on the part of many knowledgeable breeders to produce fine dogs, come into play in the selection of a puppy. The temperamental differences between one breed and the next are a very personal preference with which the knowledgeable, prospective dog owner can identify in advance of making a selection. As several psychologists have pointed out, time and time again the selection of a particular dog breed is at least to some extent a statement of self-identity, be this statement a conscious or a subconscious one. A complete mismatch, especially one caused by unnecessary ignorance, is an unfortunate development for both the person and the dog.

I recommend the use of this book by those who are already considering the possibility of acquiring a guard dog. Read the book carefully and give equal consideration to each of the breeds discussed. Until you have finished the book, looked at the photographs contained therein, and hopefully made it a point to see living, well-bred examples of as many of the breeds represented here as possible, try to dispel any preferences for or prejudices against any of these breeds that you may already have.

If this book leaves its readers with no other message than "the time to investigate a few breeds carefully is *before* one makes a selection of a dog," it will be a useful contribution. If it informs its readers about the physical and temperamental characteristics of many breeds, some of which the reader has never given consideration, it will have fulfilled its intention.

That's me in the Tosa T-shirt holding a 135-pound male Bordeaux Dogue alongside Wendy Norris and one of her bitches. Both animals belong to Steve and Wendy Norris.

If the prospects of a dog like this Fila coming at you don't send a shiver up your spine, you certainly don't scare easily. This is Ch. Ébano do Sobrado, owned by Canil Vila Maria.

PRELIMINARY CONSIDERATIONS

Man-stopping Guard Dogs: Why Should You Own One?

The term *man-stopper*, used in reference to dogs, has been around for a long time; and this book is not the first place in which it has been used in print. As the term implies, a man-stopper is a dog possessing both the temperament and physical ability to stop a human intruder by inflicting such serious bodily harm as to render further advance physically impossible. Surely such a description makes these dogs sound dangerous, if not downright evil, to the average reader. Perhaps the average reader will also question the motives of any person who would want to own a dog with this ability.

There is no need to question the discretion of owning such a dog, however. Because someone's family dog is more powerful than the average person is no reason to worry that it intends to dominate everyone it meets. Virtually every dog has the physical ability to hurt someone in an

This placid German Shepherd is a very effective guardian of a liquor store in New York City.

all-out attack, but percentages indicate that not many do. The reason is that dogs in general like people and have absolutely no desire to harm any person. The willingness to do harm to people does not increase with a dog's physical ability to do so.

Concerning the motives of people who want to own a man-stopping guard dog, I must admit that I have observed a tendency on the part of some seemingly paranoid persons to build a defense against an imagined enemy. Does their paranoia suggest that anyone who feels compelled to defend oneself is also paranoid? Being reasonably well protected against potential intrusion upon one's home is a very practical concern in today's world. An awareness of the possibility that one's property may be intruded upon and one's personal safety jeopardized is hardly evidence of paranoia. Such intrusion is not occasional, especially in urban and suburban areas where it is an embedded fact of life. It is those among us who

see no need to provide some defense against the possibility of intrusion who are being impractical, not the other way around. Keeping an effective guard dog is one method of providing such protection.

A guard dog is not the final word in defense, however. As much of a deterrent against crime as a well-trained guard dog may be, it is as vulnerable as a person is to being shot by an intruder; and secondly, it may not always be home.

Some years ago, I brought my trained American Pit Bull Terrier to my aged father's house to keep him company while my mother was vacationing in Vermont. The first day the two were alone together, my father took the dog for a walk. The house was burglarized before the walk was over . . . that's New York City for you! Do such examples render guard-dog ownership useless? Not at all.

While the possibility exists that one's home will be invaded by an intruder who kicks down the front door and runs in shooting, this is very unlikely to happen. Burglars tend to avoid breaking into homes in which they will be attacked immediately by an able defender. With so many homes to burglarize, it makes no sense for an intruder to choose the one home in which his or her safety will be in jeopardy.

It is possible that one's home will be burglarized while one is out walking the dog; however, if your dog is at home, he is on

An uncropped Doberman doing his job. The Dobie is one of the very few breeds that I feel looks better with cropped ears. Photo by Sally Anne Thompson.

12

guard. Even if asleep, the dog's keen senses and trained instincts enable him to detect an intruder. If you and your family are home, your dog most probably will be home with you; it is at such times that a guard dog is most valuable, protecting both you and your property. Most of the time when no one is home, the dog is there alone; at these times, the dog offers the sole protection of your property in your absence. In general, it is very reasonable to say that a well-trained man-stopping dog offers your home quality protection coupled with a strong deterrent effect; whether or not you feel it is all the protection you need cannot take away from its proven value.

At this point I have used the term *man-stopping dog* and the term *guard dog* a number of times. I have already explained that the term *man-stopper* refers to a dog that can literally stop a man. An explanation of the terms *guard dog* and *defense dog* is also in order. Throughout the course of this book, the term *guard dog* is used very loosely to describe any dog that is used for the protection of one's person and home. Other people use this term in a much more specific sense. Many dog trainers, for example, will object to my use of the term *guard dog* as a catch-all term. They explain that, properly defined, a dog trained for personal protection should be labeled a *personal protection dog* or possibly an *attack dog*. They

argue that *guard dog* should be reserved for dogs trained to guard property and *watch dog* to have yet another meaning.

I do not object to anyone's use of more specific terminology than is used here, and I am sure that among dog trainers such specific terminology can be very useful. It is my feeling that the vast majority of my readers are more concerned with securing a dog that is versatile, one that will understand when to guard the house against intruders and when to guard its family against attack on the street. (Not only is it possible to train a dog to do both of these things, but it will often come naturally to a dog if he has been chosen carefully and selected while still a puppy.) The use of the term *guard dog* to refer to a dog that can do both of these things will serve our purpose well. I would

The Rottweiler is gaining popularity in leaps and bounds these days as a guard dog and companion. Photo by Maria DiBenedetto.

have been equally satisfied using the term *watch dog*, *attack dog*, or *protection dog* in this general manner. But the use of several terms will be unecessary here; the term *guard dog* will suffice.

Probably the best way to answer the question, "Why should I own a man-stopping guard dog?" is with another question, "Why *not* own a man-stopping guard dog?" Given that you are inclined toward dog ownership and your circumstances allow you to own a dog comfortably, your guard dog first and foremost should be your family pet and companion and come with the added feature of offering serious protection as well.

Above: **The virtually unknown Canary Dog of Spain is another of the world's great guardian breeds.**
Right: **A black Tibetan Mastiff, a moderately sized specimen of this most impressive Oriental man-stopper.**

Who Should Own a Guard Dog?

If you have never owned a dog before but are tempted to bring home a member of one of the guardian breeds for security reasons, there are a few very serious questions you should ask yourself and the other members of your family before you proceed. The most important of these questions is: Do you really want to own a dog?

We have all heard dog owners talk about what a great responsibility owning a dog of any kind is. This comment is not just a collection of words. A dog in the home is a tremendous responsibility in that it is a relatively large living thing that requires regular meals, regular walks, and some less regular care. It is also an animal that thrives upon the attention of its human family and will never be content unless it is an active part of virtually everything your family does.

Dog ownership is expensive. Compared to the cost of maintaining a dog over the course of its life, any price you will pay for a puppy is so small that it is senseless to deprive yourself of a well-bred dog because of the extra initial expense involved. Dog food and dog supplies are not cheap, and the owner of any dog must purchase them regularly. Veterinary care is also expensive, and you will be at a complete loss for alternatives to this expenditure whenever your dog becomes ill.

A home with a dog will always require more cleaning than a home without one. If you or any member of your family is fastidious with regard to cleaning habits, the regular behavior of a dog may be downright repulsive to you.

A dog will never go on vacation, leaving you with a break from dog ownership. It will be home anticipating its usual attention every day of its life from the moment you bring it home. Any exceptions to this rule, i.e., you are going away on vacation and you can't bring your dog with you, will cost you boarding fees, and these will be considerable.

Do any of these words of discouragement sound difficult to you to live with? If so, you really don't want a dog of any kind; to bring one home on an experimental basis will only be unfair to the animal who will eventually be evicted from his

A cute American Bulldog pup. This is Steve LeClerc's Tyson at four months of age.

Where a good Rottie is involved, "Beware of Dog" is a serious warning. This watchdog weighed in at 110 pounds at the age of nine months. Photo by Maria DiBenedetto.

home, cast out of his family, and become unnecessarily expensive and burdensome to you.

But suppose you have had a dog before and you are well aware of the downside of dog ownership, or you haven't had a dog before but you are certain that dog ownership will suit your lifestyle fine, should you select your new dog from among the guardian breeds?

The dogs discussed in this book are tough animals. They have been selectively bred for

many generations to display dominance over most people, other dogs, and other animals around them. They have also been selectively bred to remain loyal and devoted to a dominant master.

To admit to yourself that you are not the kind of person that is at all motivated to be constantly expressing dominance over your pet dog is not to admit to any weakness on your part. It is wise to question yourself about the level of dominant behavior you normally express, as you go about your everyday life, before you select the breed of dog for you. This is not to be confused with the expression of a pseudo-macho attitude but must be a genuine feeling of security in your role as master of the dog. This feeling of genuine dominance over the dog will be very important as the dog begins to reach maturity and starts to question instinctively its own position in the dominance hierarchy of the household. A lack of dominance on your part will create an empty space in the hierarchy that an instinctively dominant dog will unconsciously fill. Once this happens, it will be difficult (usually impossible) to convince fully the dog that it made a mistake in its original assessment of you. It will continually assert its perceived dominance over you—and this is not a desirable situation. Furthermore, it can be downright dangerous.

Forcing yourself into the master role can never work. A dominant personality type expresses itself subtly and constantly, and the demands of the role are impossible to meet for anyone who is not instinctively inclined. If the large, obviously powerful, naturally dominant breed that you have selected could someday intimidate you with its temperament and strength, you have selected the wrong breed. You need a breed that normally does not seek to establish dominance over its human family. This will generally render you an unsuitable candidate for the ownership of a man-stopper. Again, if you are unsure of your own ability to deal with a dominant dog, experimentation is not recommended, as it can often develop into an unpleasant situation for both the owner

and the dog.

On the contrary, if you are certain of your own ability to dominate your dog but you are so aware of this tendency to dominate that you make a conscious effort to avoid expressing it, your relationship with a dominant dog is the wrong place for you to practice this avoidance strategy. Allow yourself to dominate your dog, but never confuse an expression of dominant behavior with abuse or cruelty to the animal in any way. Expressing dominance should never take the form of physical abuse.

In addition to the temperamental suitability of the owner, the practical question of physical suitability should also be taken into consideration. Remember that even a well-trained dog that respects its owner is still an animal after all. All of the breeds discussed in

Many think of the Anatolian Shepherd Dog as an effective guardian. Owner, Sarah Avery.

17

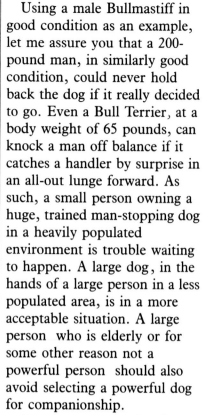

This big Rottie apparently loves his boss. Photo by Maria DiBenedetto.

this book are relatively large and strong dogs. Some of these breeds are huge and tremendously powerful. The possibility always exists that your dog will misinterpret a situation while being walked down the street or become angered in a confrontation with another dog. Even experienced owners of some of these breeds have never experienced an all-out tug-of-war with their dog; due to the dog's respect for the person on the other end of the leash, it may never have pulled in earnest.

Using a male Bullmastiff in good condition as an example, let me assure you that a 200-pound man, in similarly good condition, could never hold back the dog if it really decided to go. Even a Bull Terrier, at a body weight of 65 pounds, can knock a man off balance if it catches a handler by surprise in an all-out lunge forward. As such, a small person owning a huge, trained man-stopping dog in a heavily populated environment is trouble waiting to happen. A large dog, in the hands of a large person in a less populated area, is in a more acceptable situation. A large person who is elderly or for some other reason not a powerful person should also avoid selecting a powerful dog for companionship.

Once you are certain of your temperamental and physical suitability for guard dog ownership, and once you are certain that you are truly in the market for a dog, the question really becomes, "Why not own a man-stopping guard dog?" A guard dog is really just a dog that is able to perform the function of stopping an intruder in his tracks when called upon to do so. The companionship and affection that one is looking for in a companion dog are just as available in a guard dog as in any other canine. Remember that it is your dominance and your desire to own a dog that are of primary importance in your decision to bring home a guardian-bred dog.

The Guard Dog and the Family

Probably the greatest of all misconceptions about effective guardian breeds is the general belief that they are not one's best choice for a family dog. It is my opinion that a guard dog is a companion dog first—its willingness and ability to stop an intruder are always secondary considerations.

Attributes such as suspicion of strangers, aggression towards intruders, and the ability to bring an attacker down are all important; however, any dog that is too aggressive and intimidating to its owner is a serious problem and should be treated as such. The most capable of all man-stopping guard dogs should also be a fine companion dog and, if it is not, its suitability as a dependable guard dog should also be questioned.

There is, however, a difference between a good companion dog and a good

Above: **A large Mastiff dog in great shape. Owner, Richard Gemelski.** *Below:* **My beautiful son Daniel with a Pit Bull pup in our back yard.**

family dog. For example, I once had an aggressive purebred guard dog that was as docile as a lamb with me. Everything was fine until the day I got married and the dog began to snarl at my wife whenever I left the house. This was the finest companion dog I ever knew, but you sure couldn't call him a family dog. Things become even more complicated when you bring

that has just killed a child. The difference between the two, as drastic as it might be, lies in part in the initial selection of the dog.

Not every breed is a wise choice as a family dog. Among the guardian breeds, some are normally excellent children's dogs, especially when they have been raised with children. Others are not the best choice as a dog for kids. Exactly the

Contrary to all the bad news we hear about Pit Bulls that have been raised to be uncontrollably vicious, a well-socialized Pit Bull can really develop a bond to a young owner. Owner, the Freemans.

children, especially young children, into the picture.

Owning a dog and having a child at the same time can be one of the most rewarding experiences imaginable. It can also be one of the most horrifying. I have seen my own two-year-old son wrestling in the yard with our family dog, each of them having the time of his life; and I have been to the A.S.P.C.A. shelter to identify positively the breed of a dog

same is true of the non-guardian breeds. In fact, the most innocent and harmless looking dog from the non-protective breeds could be the least suitable dog of all for a family with young children.

From among the guardian breeds, one would be hard pressed to raise a well-bred dog from early puppyhood with children and have it mature to be a dangerous dog around any member of the family. A child that has been raised with a puppy will usually not be intimidated by the dog when the dog has reached full maturity. By the same token, a dog that has been playing with children all of its adult life will generally not become nervous if the play gets a little rougher than it would with an adult.

Any rough-housing between children and dogs should always be supervised by an adult. Even so, anyone who has made the decision to bring a puppy into a home with young children should not feel that it is necessary to avoid selecting that pup from among the guardian breeds.

Bringing a puppy home to the family should always involve a considerable amount of research and thought. I strongly recommend reading a few books, beginning with this one, that deal with the subject of the various breeds and their temperaments. Chatting with a few knowledgeable breeders shouldn't do you any harm; but bear in mind that I don't think I have ever spoken to any breeder or enthusiast of any breed who has freely admitted that his breed is a terrible choice as a family dog or even a children's dog. Breeders of fine dogs are usually people who love their dogs and, as such, they view their dogs as being very lovable. Fully believing that theirs is a lovable breed, it is not easy for most breeders to recognize their breed's limitations; therefore, a breeder's praise for his or her

dogs is usually an honest, if sometimes misleading, appraisal rather than an intentional act of deception. The result, however, can be the same, so a word of caution is in order here.

Suppose you are a family of two with grown children (who have moved out) or with none at all. While your process of selection may be a bit easier by not having to consider which breeds have the best reputations with children, it has not been eliminated altogether. A person who does not become easily intimidated by powerful dogs must always consider those around him who will also be living with this dog. A dog

My son Alexander with an incredibly powerful American Staffordshire Terrier named Spike. He's my pride and joy—and that wasn't a bad dog either.

PRELIMINARY CONSIDERATIONS

Here's a breed I've never known personally—the Beauçeron of France. I hear good things about these dogs. Owner, Castle Rock Kennels.

that will quickly learn to respect one member of the family may walk all over another member for no better reason than that one person is more comfortable around dogs. A dog that is more easily dominated might be a better choice for a family dog than some of the more dominant breeds.

Even if neither member of a family of two is intimidated by dogs, the very size and the physical strength of a dog could easily be too much for a person to handle. It is my opinion that it is a mistake to own a very large, powerful, and aggressive dog in a densely populated (urban) environment, as man cannot safely control a very powerful dog that has decided to move. For example, while an aggressive two-hundred-pound Italian Mastiff or a Japanese Tosa dog may be controllable in the hands of a large and powerful person in a suburban or rural environment, any trainer can assure you that when one of their dogs decides to lunge, a strong, two-hundred-fifty-pound man will be unable to control the dog on a crowded street. Be wary of allowing such a large dog to be walked by a smaller member of the household.

Compromises can be made. I owned a Bullmastiff in a suburban area. In such a

situation, I felt confident that I could control my dog. I do sometimes depend upon my wife to care for a dog. I do not necessarily feel confident that she can control the animal if the dog decides to take off. The solution for us is that we have a fairly large, fenced yard. I walk the dog. My wife lets the dog go into the yard.

Do not avoid the guardian breeds if you are in the market for a guard dog, but choose your family dog carefully. Use your own discretion. A well-chosen family dog is the perfect complement to an otherwise well-balanced family. No family needs a dog that is beyond the control of any member of that family.

A good Boxer is usually a great choice for a home with children. Owner, Richard Tomita. Photo by Isabelle Français.

PURCHASING AND SELECTION

Opposite: What a beautiful animal the Doberman can be. Ch. D'Mascus Sambuca v. Alisaton. Owners, Mary Manning and Charles Guardascione.

Above: My friend Wendy Norris with some appealing Bordeaux Dogue pups.

Where to Buy a Dog and How Much to Spend?

There is no sure-fire formula that will guarantee the quality of a dog based upon how much you spend for it. The general rule of thumb assuring us that we "get what we pay for" really does not apply to the purchase of a dog. There are a few generalizations that are valid, however, and it helps to be

This Bullmastiff is a real cutie, but they sure can go through awkward stages at times too.

part of the customer. Time and time again I have seen legitimately well-trained guard dogs respond like protection machines to their trainer, only to be sold for a high price to a new owner, to whom the dog will not respond at all. One must keep in mind that these dogs are not protection machines; rather, they have their own personalities and, in keeping with their own individuality, they will respond differently to different people. I have always believed that if a person can comfortably handle a trained dog and make that dog respond to him, then that person can undoubtedly train his or her own dog as the dog develops from puppyhood to adulthood. If you are determined to purchase a previously trained dog,

aware of them before we set out to buy a guard dog.

A trained dog will always cost more than a puppy or an untrained dog of the same breed. The more completely trained a dog is, i.e., from basic obedience training to advanced protection training, the more a dog will cost. The only exception to this rule is, in the case of a well-trained but old dog. For the obvious reasons, a well-trained ten-year-old dog is not normally worth much money to a prospective dog purchaser.

A great deal of time and effort on the part of a very experienced trainer is generally involved in the creation of a well-trained guard dog. As such, any trainer who has made this investment of time and effort in a dog must command a high price for the animal in order to make his investment worthwhile. This does not mean, however, that the high cost of the dog in question is a worthwhile investment on the

however, I strongly recommend handling the dog yourself before any purchase is made and being absolutely certain that the dog will respond sufficiently to you. Do not fall for the line that the dog will eventually respond to you as it grows to know you. It may, but it very well may not.

Puppies are sometimes sold by trainers along with an agreement that the initial price of the puppy will be reasonable, but a training contract, which is quite expensive, will go into effect as the pup matures. Such an agreement is a useless one to the buyer, as no one can guarantee the future temperament of the dog. One can purchase another such puppy elsewhere without being bound to a training contract.

Whether you are in the market for a trained or an untrained dog, you will soon learn that different breeds command different prices. Such price differences are not usually based on any sound ground. A very well-bred puppy of one breed may be relatively inexpensive to buy, while an equally well-bred pup of another breed may be astronomically expensive. One current example lies in the comparison of the American Pit Bull Terrier and the Doberman Pinscher. For no valid reason, one can purchase a well-bred Pit Bull for about half the price of an equally well-bred Doberman Pinscher. You may object that the much greater popularity of the Doberman accounts for the difference in price, but the fact of the matter is that such breeds as the Tosa,

A litter of young Canary Dogs around lunch time.

and the Bullmastiff, or the Neapolitan Mastiff are more expensive and in less demand generally than the Pit Bull or the Doberman.

Essentially, the difference in price between one breed and another depends upon how

organized the breeders of the breed in question are. If breeders fix their prices at casually agreed upon levels, then the cost of the breed will remain high. Where a lack of such organization exists, and especially where price wars develop, prices will plummet. This does not mean that a well-bred Pit Bull is a less valuable dog than a well-bred Doberman. If you are equally attracted to each breed, you can save yourself some money without compromising on quality by buying a puppy of a generally less expensive breed.

Even among breeders of any one breed (including those which are being produced by the most well organized of breeders) one can never be sure that spending more will ensure the acquistion of a well-bred dog. Those breeders who are breeding the finest dogs tend to be aware of the quality of their dogs; therefore, their prices are often considerably higher. Breeders of the same breed who are producing lesser dogs are not always willing to admit the inferiority of their dogs, and as such, some of these lesser animals are often priced equally high. It is the purchaser's responsibility to investigate a breed before buying a dog in order to determine a breeder's credentials. As a rule, it is a good idea to be wary of bargains and to be willing to spend more if you desire a top-quality dog.

Within a single litter of puppies, some breeders will

As huge as Tosas generally get, the breed is not short-lived as are Bullmastiffs, Neapolitans, etc. These other breeders have a lot of work to do, in my opinion.

charge more for a pup of one sex than they will for a pup of the opposite sex. Some breeders feel that if a purchaser buys a bitch rather than a dog, he can then breed the bitch and make a profit on each breeding. Some feel that a dog is potentially more profitable as a breeder than a bitch. In fact, neither sex will eventually become a "better" animal than the other. Should this problem present itself, buy whichever sex you happen to prefer.

Especially among show dogs, but also among dogs with potential as guardians, there may be a difference in price between a younger puppy, an older puppy, and a grown dog. The reasons for this are simple. A puppy, born of a great breeding of two successful show dogs or two successfully trained dogs, that shows no very obvious physical or temperamental defects at an early age is assumed by its breeder to be top quality. As

Perhaps above all, a well-raised Dobie is often an unbeatable companion dog. *Above:* Doberman owned by Lana Sniderman and Bob Krol of Canada. *Below:* Donna Blackburn's Bavlocks Angelique.

such it will command a high price. As the puppy begins to mature, however, and change in both form and temperament, some undesirable traits may begin to reveal themselves.

If a breeder has retained a pup that is six months old or older and the pup is obviously too shy for guard work or is not of competitive show quality, it can no longer command the price of a younger pup that has the potential to become such a dog. Similarly, if a breeder has kept a pup out of a good litter, and, at one year of age, the dog shows great courage and willingness to protect, or great show potential, that dog is then worth much more than a young pup which may not develop as well. The choice of whether to buy the younger pup, the older pup, or the dog is yours.

I see the question of where to buy your dog as being an easy one to answer in general terms.

That is: buy your dog from a reputable dealer who has a genuine interest in dogs and is not motivated solely by financial gain. Many fanciers are involved in breeding in the spirit of competition. Their competitive spirit is satisfied only when they breed a fine dog that brings recognition to their kennel. Such recognition is difficult to achieve. Conversely, those who breed for profit are satisfied when any dog is sold. Any dog of salable quality is good enough for them. Many fine breeds have been diminished in quality because profit-motivated persons have become involved in breeding.

Again, once you have decided upon a breed, the question of where to buy your dog must involve some serious investigation on your part. This investigation should be fun and interesting as well as useful and

valuable to you. Begin your investigation by reading as many books as is practical for you, going to as many shows as possible, and talking to as many enthusiasts as you can.

A Pup or an Adult? A Male or a Female?

The age of the dog you purchase will depend largely upon your particular circumstances. Especially if you are in the market for a tough dog among the guardian breeds, it is not at all wise to bring home a full-grown animal if there are children in your family. Where children are involved, an eight-week-old pup is ideal. At such an age it is more the children's treatment of the dog that will be your concern. By the time the dog is old enough to be potentially dangerous to the kids, it will have learned its place in the family, and the children will have learned not to be intimidated by the dog.

Even among the largest breeds, a dog that has been raised with children will generally have learned to be

This bundle of fluff will one day grow up to be a full-grown, handsome Spanish Mastiff. Owner, Mrs. Elizabeth Neiderhauser.

especially gentle with kids. To see a full-grown member of any of the giant breeds is enough to make any adult wonder about the logic of bringing such a creature home, and, especially in a home that contains children, such a conclusion may seem incomprehensible. The fact of the matter is, however, that the largest of dogs will usually adjust the intensity of their roughhousing with children to become gentler than many smaller breeds.

Keep in mind, however, when you bring home a fully grown dog from the guardian breeds, that it's not only children about which one has to worry. If any member of your family, or anyone who will sometimes be responsible for the dog, is mildly nervous around such a dog, a young puppy might be the better selection for you. A young pup should not be a frightening animal to any person. As the puppy grows, people who know the dog will normally tend to view it as a harmless and helpless dependent; even when the dog is fully grown and a potential fearless man-stopper, the fact that it can bring down a powerful man will seem little

Above: **The Dogo of Argentina is potentially one of the top guard dogs in the world today. Owner, Alejandro Malter Terrada.** *Below:* **A magnificent Neapolitan Mastiff. Owner, William Zruidio.**

Housebreaking is always a consideration when selecting a dog. Boxer pup owned by Richard Tomita. Photo by Isabelle Francais.

more than a positive asset to the dog's human family.

If you are a person who lives alone or if you live with other adults who are clearly not intimidated by dogs, a fully grown guard dog can be a good selection. Puppyhood is always a problem. No dog less than six or seven months of age should ever be expected to be fully housebroken. Until a dog is five or six months of age, sometimes even older, it simply does not have the muscular control to be fully housebroken. In very basic terms, this means that if you bring home an eight-week-old puppy, you can expect to be housebreaking for three to five months. This being the case, if you are in a position to bring home a grown, fully housebroken dog, you have saved yourself a great deal of work.

In addition to some of the basic problems of puppyhood, there are practical problems that are usually undesirable. For example, not only can one not enjoy taking a nice evening

We had this Bullmastiff (Cody) for three and a half years, until cancer did him in. We miss the dog still. He was the ideal family dog.

Below: German Shepherd pup at his master's feet.

walk with a young puppy (one of my favorite pastimes), but one cannot reasonably expect any protection from a puppy. To buy an eight-week-old pup as your only dog is to assure yourself that you will not have a guard dog for at least a year. (If you already have a grown dog in the house, bringing home an adult dog that is dominant by nature can often present a big problem, as you are putting your dogs in a very awkward position. In such a situation, a puppy is a wiser choice.) I know trainers who will begin the attack training of a dog at seven or eight months of age, but I strongly advise against such practices. No dog should be attack-trained until it has clearly reached maturity. This can range from an age of 12 to 24 months, depending

upon the nature and breed of the dog. If it is your aim to have an effective guard dog on the premises quickly, the possibility of procuring a grown dog should be investigated.

In the same way that a grown dog may come complete with many good habits, it may also come complete with many bad ones. Bad habits can sometimes be very difficult to break, while a bit of early puppyhood training will usually last throughout a dog's entire life. Such good habits are invaluable. The important thing here is that, if you have decided upon an adult dog, be very sure to get one that already behaves in the manner that you want. It is often easier to simply buy a puppy and train it yourself. Personally, I have had great success both ways, so I have no bones to pick in either direction, but caution is always advisable.

In terms of proper guardian temperament, one is always taking a chance (although these chances can be greatly minimized) in choosing a puppy as opposed to an adult. A grown dog that has demonstrated its courage and guarding ability to you is a sure-fire guard dog for a future owner who can handle it. No eight-week-old puppy is a sure-fire future guard dog. You can minimize your chances of choosing a puppy that will mature without sufficient courage and aggression for serious guard work by careful selection; but even among the

most well bred of the guardian breeds the possibility of finding a natural born "sweetheart" always exists. This is not to give the impression that selecting a future guard dog from puppyhood is a very risky business. So as not to discourage you, let me assure you that finding a well-bred Pit Bull pup, for example, that will not eventually develop into a suitable guardian (if it has been properly raised) is about as common as a snow storm in July. But some breeds are not as sure-fire as others, and, even among the best, true courage is so difficult to firmly implant in a genetic line that no breeder can ever claim to provide exclusively truly courageous guard-dog puppies.

In order to begin to understand why this is so, you should stop for a minute to consider exactly what it is that we are asking of a guard dog, and to compare the average guard dog's natural level of aggression and courage to that of the average person. How many people have you known who were temperamentally suited for the job of being on

A Kuvasz can be a very useful guardian, and the breed is very good looking too.

35

Right: A Fila Brasileiro pup. I think either you like the way these dogs look or you really don't. Owner, Marilyn Harned. *Below:* A beautiful white Akita. Akitas make great bear hunters too. Owner, Marietta H. Jones.

the alert for any intruder at all times and for being completely willing to attack and fight to the death anything that will ever pose a threat to his home and especially his human family? I don't think I have ever heard of any such person and I doubt that I ever will. Despite the many generations of very selective breeding practices that have brought the guardian dog breeds to their current levels of suitability for guard work, inheritance is much too unpredictable for any breeder to produce ideal puppies every time. If you want to be sure of getting a good guard dog, purchasing a proven adult is definitely an option that is worth considering.

The question of whether to choose a male (dog) or a female (bitch) as a guard dog really amounts to little more than a matter of personal choice. Many meaningless prejudices come into play when such a decision is to be made. Most

Sequel

dog enthusiasts will express a preference for either a dog or a bitch. I am no different from everyone else in this respect, and I have my own preference too. Personally, I prefer to own a male. My reasoning is that when I am in search of a guard dog, the male will ultimately offer more of the features I'm looking for. In my opinion, the male is the better choice for guard work because it is bigger, stronger, frequently more aggressive, and presents more of an imposing figure than a female of the same breed and quality. Others will argue that the female bonds more closely to its family and is more inclined to protect its family than a male. They will say the female is big and strong enough and presents enough of an imposing figure to get the job done. As such, they will tell you it is the all-around better choice.

I would like to advise you that it is all meaningless, really, and that either is as good as the other for guardian purposes; but as I've told you, I do have my own prejudices here. One way or the other, either the dog or the bitch can become an excellent guardian, and, while many of us have our preferences, neither choice is a wrong one. Select whichever sex you happen to prefer. If your dog does not become a good guardian, it will not be because you selected the wrong sex.

Two Tosa pups being cuddled in Japan. It sure looks like the Japanese like these dogs.

Steve LeClerc of Indian Hy Kennels (Hampden, Massachusetts) with one of his great stud dogs.

THE

GUARD DOGS:

AN EXPLANATION

A smart
Anatolian.
These are
quick-
thinking,
quick-acting
guardians.

The following is intended to introduce the reader to a number of breeds of dog. These dogs are among the finest guardians in the world. In addition to the willingness to perform the task of guard work, members of these breeds can be considered to be serious man-stoppers; i.e., they have the physical ability to dispatch a human attacker.

Some of the following breeds are more physically suited to stop intruders, others more temperamentally. Some are well suited, both physically and temperamentally, but are unsuited for apartment life or even indoor life. In order to learn the inherent nature of the breeds, especially if you are unfamiliar with a particular one, you must read the subsequent sections carefully. In fact, I would prefer that anyone who intends to choose a breed largely on the basis of

A strong and handsome Pit Bull Terrier. These animals require quality owners because they are great dogs. This is Peg's George W. of Kemo Kennels. Photo by Peggy Allen.

what this book has to say read all of the breed sections carefully and not make a selection until he/she is at least somewhat familiar with each of the breeds discussed here.

As I have said before, I would prefer this to be one of at least a few books that a prospective guard dog owner will read before making any selection. It is important that you ultimately select a breed that is temperamentally suited to you. The more you read on the subject of breed temperament characteristics, the more you will know. I have long since found that no one book on the subject of dogs (or any other subject for that matter) contains all the information you will need to know before making a detailed decision; and I am not so vain as to feel that this book is the one shining exception to that rule. I would prefer that my readers use this book as an encyclopedic introduction to the breeds discussed and to make their final decision based primarily upon actual personal observation of dogs and discussion with breeders. Again, one must be careful, for breeders are not known for their willingness to say negative things about a breed they love.

I feel very confident that this

book offers a very accurate picture of man-stopping guard dogs in general, and of the specifics on the breeds discussed herein. If you are one of those people who prefers to make rash decisions in such an area as buying a dog, I firmly believe that a thorough reading of this book will give you enough information to make a worthwhile selection. If this book does nothing but that, I will be happy you decided to read it.

Once you are aware of the breeds that I have chosen to discuss, you will probably wonder why I am not discussing one breed or

A typical Bull Terrier. Photo by Isabelle Français. Owners, Tom and Irene Lecki.

THE GUARD DOGS: AN EXPLANATION

Right: **Bull Terrier photo by the author.** *Below:* **A brindle Fila Brasileiro.**

another. Many of us know someone, somewhere, who has a Weimaraner, a Chesapeake Bay Retriever, or another dog that is an exceptional guard dog and "sure looks like it could bring a man down if it had to." Believe me, I am aware of such dogs, but a few terrific dogs do not make a man-stopping guard *breed*. The breeds discussed were chosen for discussion

among so many because of the extreme likelihood that their members will mature to be highly suited for guard work and possess man-stopping ability.

There is most definitely a great difference among breeds in regard to the suitability for guard work. Percentage-wise, anyone in the market for a man-stopper will have a much greater chance of finding one among the breeds discussed here than among virtually all of the remainder of the world's pure breeds. For this reason, it is essential that, if you are in search of a puppy that will mature to express the proper combination of temperamental and physical characteristics for guard work, you must begin your search by looking at the right breeds. The breeds discussed in this book are the right breeds. Any breed exemption is quite intentional on my part and based upon my belief that the breed in question does not rank with these others in the area of general guardian ability.

Differences in ability among these breeds are sometimes a consideration to be reckoned with. These differences are discussed in the breed sections. All breeds discussed are noteworthy for their man-stopping guardian ability. If you make your selection of a pup based upon some serious thought, the likelihood that you will secure a fine guard dog from among any of these breeds is great. With some well-directed reading, some meaningful discussion, and a little bit of effort, you will be able to choose a great companion and a fine family protector that will be with you for many years to come.

A downright monumental Spanish Mastiff. Photo by Carlos Salas Melero.

THE PIT BULL/
THE AMERICAN STAFFORDSHIRE TERRIER

Opposite: The expression of the American Pit Bull Terrier cannot be mistaken. Photo by Isabelle Français. Owner, Lynne Ferguson. *Left:* A wonderful American Staffordshire Terrier winning a show. This is a breed that will love its master to the end. This is Ch. Ledge Rock's Kopper Korn. Owners, Ernest and Ruth Prehn.

Suppose that you are a city apartment dweller or own a small home with little room to spare, and you have decided that it is time to get a guard dog with plenty of man-stopping ability. On the one hand, you want a great companion dog with a temperament that is aggressive toward intruders and

THE PIT BULL/THE AM. STAFF.

has actual biting power that is absolutely tremendous. On the other hand, it just isn't feasible for you to own a huge dog in a small home. A huge dog would always be in your way and it would always be frustrated due to the limited space. You wish that there was a breed that combined the speed, power and determination of the best of the man-stopping dogs with the suitability of a small- to medium-sized apartment dog.

Rest assured, because such a breed exists.

The American Pit Bull Terrier or Pit Bull is known far and wide to be the gamest and most capable fighting dog known to modern man. It is probably the gamest and most capable fighting dog that has ever existed as well. When the spectator sport of bullbaiting was outlawed in England by an act of Parliament in 1835, former bullbaiters turned their attention to the newly popular sport of organized dogfighting, (the pitting of one powerful dog against another).

While the "Bulldogge" of the time was very positively adapted to baiting the bull, fighting-dog breeders soon discovered that a cross between the Bulldogge and any of the game and relatively powerful terriers of the day produced a game, powerful, agile and smaller, more capable opponent in the dog pits. These bull-and-terrier dogs rose to great

THE PIT BULL/THE AM. STAFF.

heights of popularity among dog fighters and soon were the only fighting dogs used by the pit-fighting fraternity of Western Europe. As the only bull-and-terrier dogs used as pit fighters, these dogs were bred only to other dogs of the same cross. A purebred type was eventually fixed as a result of this careful selection for specific functional qualities.

With the emigration of people from Great Britain to the United States, the bull-and-terrier breed found its way across the Atlantic. Dogfighting became as popular in North America as it was in Western Europe and, as the bull-and-terrier continued to reign supreme in their performance in the pit, the dogs became popular in the United States as well. With time, the American dogs began to take on a unique appearance. This was due not only to the fact that many different populations of bull-and-terrier fighters were being blended together to produce the American version of the breed but also to the fact that American dog fighters expressed a preference for a somewhat larger dog. Indeed, the American bull-and-terrier dog was generally a larger animal.

When the American Kennel Club was established in 1884, it failed to register this fighting dog, even though the breed was well known at the time. It is believed that in recognition of the value of the breed and of the need to preserve it as a

registered purebred, C.Z. Bennett established the United Kennel Club in 1898 for the sole purpose of registering these dogs, which at the time were being called by a variety of names such as American Bulldog, American Bull Terrier, Pit Bull, Yankee Terrier, etc. The breed grew in popularity not only among pit fighters, but also among dog lovers in general.

It was not until 1935, when "Pete" of the *Our Gang* comedy series brought the breed further public recognition, that the American Kennel Club saw fit

Unless you know the dog well, getting this close to an angry Pit Bull can be dangerous. Sequan Invictas undergoes attack training. Photo by Richard F. Stratton.

I guess we all have our favorites in life, and for me, these dogs are it. What a good looking dog this is! American Staffordshire Terrier. Photo by Isabelle Français. Owner, Sigrid Reisiger.

to accept it into its stud book. The A.K.C. chose the name Staffordshire Terrier (after Staffordshire, England) for its new registrants, and the A.K.C. Staffordshire Terrier and the U.K.C. Pit Bull Terrier coexisted comfortably.

Both the Staffordshire Terrier and the Pit Bull Terrier remain members of their respective kennel clubs today, with the minor change that each club has since chosen to

Opposite (top): A handsome pair of Am Staffs looking undeniably sweet. Owners, Ron Tucker and Rita A. Pauciello. *Opposite (bottom):* Von Herpen's "Red Boy" pauses from morning exercise.

add the title "American" to the beginning of its breed name. Although, as we have seen, the A.K.C. and the U.K.C. Bull Terriers have identical origins, they have to some extent grown apart over the years. Two factors are responsible for the divergence of both the appearance and the temperament of these dogs. First, the Staffordshire Terriers registered by the American Kennel Club became almost exclusively show dogs as opposed to fighters. The selection by breeders for the esthetically pleasing rather than

functionally capable representatives of the breed soon modified the appearance as well as the performance of the A.K.C. dogs. Even as the U.K.C. became more and more interested in the show aspect of the Pit Bull Terrier breed, the differences between the written show standard for the Pit Bull Terrier and the Staffordshire Terrier further contributed to the divergence in the appearance of these dogs and very possibly to the divergence in their relative functional value as well.

In spite of the differences between the modern-day

Above: **A well-trained American Pit Bull Terrier competing in a United Kennel Club obedience trial.** *Below:* **The well-socialized Pit Bull is a more versatile dog than many realize. Basically this is a breed that truly wants to do whatever you want it to. This is Hammonds's "Bruno" the Beggar. Photo by Richard F. Stratton.**

American Pit Bull Terrier and the American Staffordshire Terrier, either of these dogs will prove capable and willing to serve well at guard work. Curiously, less than a decade ago, it was believed by many who knew the breed—but did not know it very well—that the Pit Bull was such a people-loving dog that the breed was useless for serious guard work. In much of my own earlier writing, I advised my readers not to believe this foolish myth, as the Pit Bull I owned at the time—as well as numerous others I knew well—had long since proven to me that the breed loved only its family and the friends of its family and would oppose any enemy of its family with a ferocity that was unprecedented in the world of dogs.

I am compelled not to allow this chapter to end without advising my readers not to believe the latest myth about the Pit Bull breed. It is a myth that germinated in the minds of those who are ignorant where purebred dogs are concerned but who take a firm position as if there were some intelligence backing it up. It is the myth that the Pit Bull is a vicious animal by nature and, therefore, dangerous and unreasonable to own. Many have gone so far as to suggest that they are not even dogs in the common sense of the word, but rather some horrible cross between dog and killer beast. The myth has spread so far that some areas of the U.S. have even outlawed the breed!

I wish it were needless to say

What a glorious smile! Photo by Isabelle Français.

that this latest myth is based upon nothing more than a large dose of ignorance combined with a little dose of stupidity. As the myth has been so widely accepted, let me state that the American Pit Bull Terrier and the American Staffordshire Terrier are exceptional dogs because they are so very willing and able to become the dogs you wish them to be. Raise them to be gentle and they will be gentle. Raise them to be vicious and they will be vicious. Raise them to be loving companions and terrific protectors of your home and family— children included— and that is exactly what these dogs will be. Problems lie not in the breed but in the people who have become attracted to the breed in very recent years. For my money, I have never known a breed that so fits my own image of the perfect dog. I will tell you, of all dogs, I love these dogs the most.

Standard for the American Pit Bull Terrier

HEAD—Medium length. Bricklike in shape. Skull flat and widest at the ears, with prominent cheeks free from wrinkles.

Muzzle—Square, wide and deep. Well pronounced jaws, displaying strength. Upper teeth should meet tightly over lower teeth, outside in front.

Ears—Cropped or uncropped (not important). Should set high on head, and be free from wrinkles.

Eyes—Round. Should set far apart, low down on skull. Any color acceptable.

Nose—Wide open nostrils. Any color acceptable.

Neck—Muscular. Slightly arched. Tapering from shoulder to head. Free from looseness of skin.

SHOULDERS—Strong and muscular, with wide sloping shoulder blades.

BACK—Short and strong. Slightly sloping from withers to rump. Slightly arched at loins, which should be slightly tucked.

CHEST—Deep, but not too

Right: A big, strong, red Pit Bull. The A.K.C. doesn't like this color in their breed—I love it. *Below:* A docile family of Pit Bulls. Photo by Isabelle Français.

A classic "I'm content and all's well" Pit Bull facial expression.

broad, with wide sprung ribs.

RIBS—Close, well sprung, with deep back ribs.

TAIL—Short in comparison to size. Set low and tapering to a fine point. Not carried over back. Bobbed tail not acceptable.

LEGS—Large, round boned, with straight, upright pasterns, reasonably strong. Feet to be of medium size. Gait should be light and springy. No rolling or pacing.

THIGH—Long with muscles developed. Hocks down straight.

COAT—Glossy. Short and stiff to the touch.

Color—Any color or markings permissible.

WEIGHT—Not important. Females preferred from thirty to fifty pounds. Males from thirty-five to sixty pounds.

Keep in mind when reading through the above standard that it is intentionally free of the rigidity we will see in the A.K.C.'s standard for the American Staffordshire Terrier, as the Pit Bull Terrier was developed as a performance animal and not for show.

Get a look at the musculature of this fine-looking white Pit Bull. He looks like he's been exercising. "Bo" weighs in at 80 pounds.

Left: A fine American Staffordshire Terrier owned by Ron Klopper. *Below:* A typical, good-looking Pit Bull. This is Grider's Pit Colonel.

THE AKITA

Although such factors as temperament, functional ability, size, overall suitability for guard work and the specific history of a breed must be considered, even the most ardent dog enthusiast will eventually admit that he is simply partial to the appearance of one breed or another. While appearance alone should never be the sole determinant in the selection of a breed, one may as well select a body style that one prefers from among the many different quality breeds available. Until only a few years ago, dog enthusiasts who preferred for esthetic reasons to own one of the northern breeds were extremely hard pressed to combine this preference with a desire to own a guard dog. While such breeds as the Alaskan Malamute and the Siberian Husky might be beautiful, powerful, courageous, and docile family

Opposite: The Akita is everyone's idea of handsome. *Above:* The breed is admired for its pleasantness and trust-worthiness. Photo by Isabelle Français. Owners, Steve and Marian Lisker.

dogs, they simply do not work well as willing guard dogs at all. One northern breed, which has only been registered in the stud book of the American Kennel Club since 1973, is an exception to this rule. It combines the classic look of the northern dogs with the functional qualities of a man-stopper. This breed is the Akita.

The Akita-Inu (Akita Dog), or simply the Akita, is a large breed of Japanese origin. Of the ten purebreds registered by the Japan Kennel Club and recognized as being of Japanese origin, the Akita is one of six breeds which shares a very similar and very distinctively northern body style. These six breeds, namely (1) the Akita, (2) the Kishu Ken, (3) the Shiba, (4) the Shikoku Ken, (5) the Ainu Ken, and (6) the Kai Ken, all display a short to medium length coat with a soft undercoat, relatively small pricked ears, a tail curled over the back of the dog in typical northern breed style, a broad head, and a generalized northern breed body type. It is obvious upon seeing these dogs that all are derived from common ancestry.

The common ancestor of the Akita and the other five Akita-like Japanese breeds is a hunting dog. For this reason,

Two good Akitas apparently interested in something up there. Photo by Isabelle Français. Owners, Steve and Marian Lisker.

and also because the Akita is often employed as a big game hunter in Japan, much of the modern dog literature in the U.S. refers to the Akita as a hunting dog. In fact, while the Kishu Ken, the Shikoku Ken, the Ainu Ken, the Kai Ken (all medium-sized dogs) and the Shiba (a small dog) are all referred to as being either primarily hunting dog/companion dog, companion dog/hunting dog or companion dog/watch dog/hunting dog by the Japan Kennel Club, only the Akita is referred to as being purely a "companion dog." This is because the history of this breed is not to be traced to the hunting fields, but rather to the dog pits of Japan. Consider the following brief history of the

Akitas come in some pretty unusual color combinations. Photo by Isabelle Français. Owner, John D'Alessio.

There aren't many things on earth cuter than an Akita pup. Photo by Isabelle Français. Owner, Edward J. Finnegan, Jr.

Akita which appears in a short booklet on Japanese breeds entitled "Japanese Dogs," written and distributed by the Japan Kennel Club. The J.K.C. says of the breed that "the Akita-Inus were originally middle-sized hunting dogs in old times in Tohoku district (northeastern section of Japan). They developed into fighting dogs from the Edo era (1600 to 1868) to the Taisho era (1912 to 1926), becoming gradually known by the name 'Akita' and are internationally spread as a large-sized breed of Japanese origin representing Japan."

While many dog enthusiasts seem to feel that hunting is a more acceptable usage for the Akita than participation in organized dogfighting, the history of the breed is unfortunately not as cooperative as these Akita enthusiasts would prefer. The fact remains, however, that the Akita is sometimes used as a big game hunter in Japan; but as teams of two dogs are normally hunted together, these teams must generally consist of a male dog and a bitch, as two of the same sex will often fight between themselves (as fighting dogs will). Even the American standard for the Akita calls for this breed to be aggressive around other dogs. When a team of two Akitas is properly trained to hunt, the dogs often become so skilled at the task that the two Akitas can bring down a bear without a shot being fired.

In any event, the Akita is a large, powerful, fearless, game breed that can become a very useful man-stopping dog. Problems do sometimes arise, however, in training these dogs for guard work. In general I have found that a mature Akita will often respond well to agitation and remember the lesson that not all people are to be trusted forever. When an Akita has been so trained, either professionally or otherwise, it is on a par with some of the best guard dogs available. The breed, however, does not always express an interest in instinctively protecting its home against intruders, and I personally know of many well-bred Akitas that are maintained as house dogs which, if the door of the house were opened wide by an intruder, would undoubtedly seize the opportunity to run out of the house and roam the streets rather than attack. The moral of this story is that the Akita can be a good man-stopping dog, but the breed is not for everyone. Don't select an Akita puppy as a future guard dog unless you are sure

of your ability to work effectively with the dog to bring out its rather deep-rooted protective nature. Also, be sure your Akita likes you. Some breeds, even the most dominant of breeds, will respond to and even require a little harmless bullying now and then if you are to establish your own dominance over them. This is not usually a good way to train an Akita. An Akita will respond to bullying by becoming aloof and more stubborn than ever. Train an Akita by making it feel that while you are always

A picture like this reminds me that I'd like to own an Akita some day. Photo by Isabelle Français. Owner, Windom Akitas.

its friend, others are not always as friendly as you. If you like the appearance of the Akita and you really want to own a northern breed, be prepared to put in more work at the beginning than you might with a less stubborn breed. The end result should be a powerful, determined, man-stopping dog.

Standard for the Akita

also characteristic of the breed.

HEAD—Massive but in balance with the body; free of wrinkle when at ease. Skull flat between ears and broad; jaws square and powerful with minimal dewlap. Head forms a blunt triangle when viewed from above. **Fault**—Narrow or snipy head.

Muzzle—Broad and full. Distance from nose to stop is to distance from stop to

The Akita's gait is described as brisk and powerful. Photo by Isabelle Français. Handler, Fran Wasserman.

GENERAL APPEARANCE—Large, powerful, alert, with much substance and heavy bone. The broad head, forming a blunt triangle, with deep muzzle, small eyes and erect ears carried forward in line with back of neck, is characteristic of the breed. The large curled tail, balancing the broad head, is

occiput as 2 is to 3.

Stop—Well defined, but not too abrupt. A shallow furrow extends well up forehead.

Nose—Broad and black. Liver permitted on white Akitas, but black always preferred.

Disqualification—Butterfly nose or total lack of pigmentation on nose.

Ears—The ears of the Akita are characteristic of the breed. They are strongly erect and small in relation to rest of head. If ear is folded forward for measuring length, tip will touch upper eye rim. Ears are triangular, slightly rounded at tip, wide at base, set wide on head but not too low, and carried slightly forward over eyes in line with back of neck. **Disqualification**—Drop

Noticeably undershot or overshot.

NECK—Thick and muscular; comparatively short, widening gradually toward shoulders. A pronounced crest blends with base of skull.

BODY—Longer than high, as 10 is to 9 in males; 11 to 9 in bitches. Chest wide and deep; depth of chest is one-half height of dog at shoulder. Ribs well sprung, brisket well developed. Level

The temperament of the breed is typically aggressive towards other dogs. Such introductions should be undertaken with caution. Owner, Dr. Sanford Paul. Photo by Ron Reagan.

or broken ears.

Eyes—Dark brown, small, deep-set and triangular in shape. Eye rims black and tight.

Lips and tongue—Lips black and not pendulous; tongue pink.

Teeth—Strong with scissors bite preferred, but level bite acceptable. **Disqualification**—

back with firmly muscled loin and moderate tuck-up. Skin pliant but not loose. **Serious faults**—Light bone, rangy body.

Forequarters—Shoulders strong and powerful with moderate layback. Forelegs heavy-boned and straight as viewed from front. Angle of pastern 15 degrees forward from vertical. **Faults**—Elbows in or out, loose shoulders. *Hindquarters*—Width, muscular development and comparable to forequarters. Upper thighs well developed. Stifle moderately bent and hocks well let down, turning neither in nor out.

One look at the faces of these dogs will tell you why so many Japanese name their Akitas "Kuma," meaning bear. Owner, Windom Akitas.

Feet—Cat feet, well knuckled up with thick pads. Feet straight ahead.

TAIL—Large and full, set high and carried over back or against flank in a three-quarter curl, full, or double curl, always dipping to below level of back. On a three-quarter curl, tip drops well down flank. Root large and strong. Tail bone reaches hock when let down. Hair coarse, straight and full, with no appearance of a plume. **Disqualification**—Sickle or uncurled tail.

COAT—Double-coated. Undercoat thick, soft, dense and shorter than outer coat. Outer coat straight, harsh and standing somewhat off body. Hair on head, legs and ears short. Length of hair at withers and rump approximately two inches, which is slightly longer than on rest of body, except tail, where coat is longest and most profuse. **Fault**—Any indication of ruff or feathering.

Color—Any color including white, brindle, or pinto. Colors are brilliant and clear and markings are well balanced with or without mask or blaze. White Akitas have no mask. Pinto has a white background with large, evenly placed patches covering head and more than one-third of body. Undercoat may be a different color from outer coat.

GAIT—Brisk and powerful with strides of moderate length. Back remains strong, firm and level. Rear legs move in line with front legs.

SIZE—Males 26 to 28 inches at the withers; bitches 24 to 26 inches. **Disqualification**—Dogs under 25 inches; bitches under 23 inches.

TEMPERAMENT—Alert and responsive, dignified and courageous. Aggressive towards other dogs.

I had an Akita's leash wrapped around my arm in the woods one day when the dog spotted a deer. Boy, did I go for a ride! Owner, Windom Akitas.

An impressive example of the breed, Dick the Bruiser.

THE AMERICAN BULLDOG

A powerful American Bulldog. Sampson is owned by Steve LeClerc.

About five years ago I wrote a book entitled *The World Of Fighting Dogs* (T.F.H. Publications, Inc., 1984). This book is essentially a chapter-by-chapter discussion of some of the lesser known dog breeds that were originally developed as fighting dogs but which then and now are very useful as companion and protection dogs. One of the breeds I

This American Bulldog is LeClerc's Pistol— 70 pounds at four years of age.

devote a chapter to in that book is the American Bulldog. To my knowledge, that chapter is, for all practical purposes, the first place in all of the world's dog literature in which the American Bulldog breed was ever discussed.

The results of that chapter and of some later writing that I did for a magazine were both negative and positive. The negative results were that many American Bulldog breeders decided that they disliked me intensely for having described the breed as I saw it rather than just fawning all over it and them by saying nothing but positive things about the breed. As a serious dog writer and enthusiast, I couldn't do that for them because the breed had a long way to go before any interested person could buy a pup confident that it would mature to be an accurate representation of the breed. Another negative result was that the very same breeders who claimed to be so upset because I had bad-mouthed the breed almost immediately raised their prices at an exorbitant rate in response to the tremendous demand for the breed that the book and the articles generated. Bear in mind that this is their profit, not mine.

The positive results of my writing about the breed were that public awareness of the American Bulldog sky-rocketed over night among dog enthusiasts throughout the U.S. and across the Atlantic. Furthermore, some serious breeders became interested in the breed and as a result I can now tell you that the overall quality of the breed has improved quite fast, and that, if one does his research carefully, quality American Bulldog stock is now available. I like these dogs and if I do say so myself I see my contribution to the preservation and development of this breed as being very substantial vis-à-vis my efforts.

To those early American Bulldog breeders who still hold a grudge and who will deny my contribution to the breed as a result, let me ask the following question: Where were you before I came into the picture, guys? Did you manage to do in forty years what I've done in five? And what did I ever ask of anyone for my contribution? Nothing! What did I get? I had

to listen to stupidity from you. That was all I ever got other than the personal satisfaction I've derived from seeing the breed grow to a level at which it has completely transcended you.

Anyway, now that I've begun by offering some background information and by seizing the opportunity to toot my own horn a little as well, let me tell you that I now have far fewer negative things to say about the American Bulldog breed than I did five years ago. While selecting a breeder should involve being every bit as discriminating as I advised in my previous book, at least now I can tell you that a thorough investigation should result in your securing a puppy that will grow to be precisely what you hoped it would be.

The American Bulldog is as truly American and as much a Bulldog as any breed that exists. For the true fancier of the Bulldogge of old, no breed on the face of the earth today will suffice like this tough-as-nails, highly spirited Bulldog. By way of description, let me assure you that the true American Bulldog should not and will not remind one of an American Staffordshire Terrier or the Pit Bull (although every ounce of that great Staff spirit is alive and well in the body of the American Bulldog). It will not remind one of the Bullmastiff (although the locomotive-like strength of the Bullmastiff is readily apparent in the American Bulldog); nor

"I like these dogs and if I do say so myself I see my contribution to the preservation and development of this breed as being very substantial vis-à-vis my efforts."

will it remind one of the Boxer (although the gladiator's history is as easy-to-read in the appearance of the American Bulldog as it is in the Boxer). Most of all, it is completely unlike that poor animal known today as the English Bulldog, or simply the Bulldog. If any comparison would be an unfair one, it would be between the great athlete that is the American Bulldog and the friendly little frog-like creature that is the Bulldog of the show ring.

The American Bulldog is a powerfully built, blocky, yet extremely athletic animal that exudes "true grit" few modern breeds still can. It is a natural guardian in that its spirit is intact and any properly bred member of this breed is as sure-fire a guardian as you will find anywhere. Having said this, let me warn you of something you may well encounter in your search for a good Bulldog.

Due to the fact that those who would outlaw the American Pit Bull Terrier generally know less about dogs than anyone you or I will ever know on a personal level, some confusion has been generated in the collective mind of the lay public as to whether or not the American Bulldog and the Pit Bull are more or less the same dog. (I am telling you they are not.) In order to keep the simple-minded, "holier-than-thou" at bay, the wisest of American Bulldog breeders are beginning to adopt the policy of describing this breed as being

totally non-aggressive.

As a result, do not be surprised if you call one of the few breeders of quality American Bulldogs in order to ask questions that are quite reasonable for anyone in the market for a potential guard dog only to hear descriptions of the breed which sound anything but attractive. I had one breeder whose efforts I seriously admire tell me he's never seen an American Bulldog that wouldn't turn and run the first time you raise your fist to it and yell in a threatening manner. If you're reading this, pal, I've got to tell you this: I've seen your dogs and you know I've seen your dogs. Anyone who can't make an effective guard dog out of any of your dogs shouldn't own a dog at all. (And I certainly hope that you don't think I don't know that!)

Once again, I am advising those among you who prefer real Bulldogs to consider the American Bulldog. Remember that it is of great importance that you select your breeder very carefully if it's a true representative of the breed that you are looking for, and that you be prepared to spend a deal of money on it.

Breeders asking a lot of money for American Bulldogs fall into two categories: the know-nothing opportunist, some of whom have been involved in American Bulldogs for a long time; and the serious breeder of quality dogs who had to pay so much initially to purchase usable breeding stock that his prices must be high simply to recoup his investment. Such breeders deserve the money asked. As much as they may deserve their price however, many fanciers of the breed are unable, if not unwilling, to shell out that much money for a dog. To you I say, price your stock now and then wait awhile. Believe me, the prices will come down as the quality stock in this country becomes more readily available.

Concerning the history of this breed, I can tell you that I have given this matter considerable thought for many years now—and I still can't tell you where the hell these dogs came from. My dilemma is this: I have seen original photographs of these dogs which date back many years. At that time they looked pretty much as they do today. That, mind you, is saying a great deal more than one can say for many of today's most highly respected American Kennel Club purebreds. If you don't believe me, try taking a look at pictures of the Bouvier des Flandres that date back some fifty-odd years and see what

LeClerc's Warhorse hanging around.

you've got.

On the other hand, the American Bulldog is now and has until now always been purely a performance animal. As such, the "purity" of the cultivated lines was at best a secondary consideration—the primary consideration always being the performance ability of the animal concerned. As such, even the most sincere of breeders saw good and fair reason to breed into their lines animals that would increase the overall performance level of the breed. So why not a little Pit Bull if the lines were game enough? Why not a little something else if the size was substantial enough? This is the way many of today's greatest

Active and robust, American Bulldogs make biddable guard dogs.

A fine American Bulldog owned by LeClerc. It's probably the best one I've ever seen.

purebreds were originally constructed. Why not accept the same breeding strategy in the case of the American Bulldog?

But again, one of the great things about getting involved in the American Bulldog just now is that: (*a*) the good dogs are damn good; and (*b*) you can come in on the ground floor and make a real contribution in your own, very essential way. I am telling you clearly: find a good American Bulldog and you've got one of the best dogs there is for anyone in search of a very trainable man-stopping guard dog.

Let me end this chapter with the following comment. I believe that the future of the American Bulldog lies in the hands of European breeders. It is the Dutch, the German, to some extent the French, and other purebred enthusiasts abroad who will ultimately isolate the best breeding stock available and who will realize its fullest potential. It is they who will not know as they buy their dogs what know-nothings have been involved in this breed until now and who will respect them for their qualities. Mark my words—it is they who will isolate the best there is to offer and help, in the long run, make a "forever" breed of these dogs. To them I say, "Go for it!"

(Incidentally, no breed standard will follow here because any meaningful standard exists only in my mind and in the collective mind of a very few breeders. As a point of interest only, see the breed standard used in my first book, *The World Of Fighting Dogs*).

THE ANATOLIAN SHEPHERD DOG

THE ANATOLIAN SHEPHERD DOG

Opposite: The Anatolian is hailed as one of Turkey's foremost guard dogs. Photo by Isabelle Français. Owner, Betty Leferve.

Above: A white Anatolian showing her pup the ins-and-outs of frog hunting. Courtesy of Hill Country Kennels.

The only meaningful way to begin any honest discussion about the Anatolian Shepherd Dog is to refer to a very unfortunate situation that has been developing for quite some time. The situation is that there is currently such intense disagreement among enthusiasts of these dogs, concerning precisely what the dogs are, that many would-be newcomers to the breed are becoming completely disillusioned with the low-level controversy and, therefore, not getting involved with the breed. I will try to explain the situation as clearly and as briefly as possible, but I must warn my readers in advance that the supposed experts on the breed cannot even come to any agreement over the question of how many breeds we are talking about when we refer to the Anatolian Shepherd Dogs. I prefer to remain impartial here, however, as I am weary of the debate. These are the facts as I understand them. You can make up your own mind as to how many breeds are involved.

The disagreement begins with the labeling of these shepherd dogs as "Anatolian." As closely as I can ascertain, they who disagree with this labeling would feel more comfortable (although would still be far from satisfied) if we referred to the dogs as being Turkish rather than Anatolian, because they feel that few people know where Anatolia is. For purposes of clarity then, the area of the world that the ancient Greeks referred to as Anatolia comprises the western peninsula of the continent of Asia, adjoining the Mediterranean Sea on the south, the Aegean Sea on the west, and the Strait of Dardanelles, the Sea of Marmara, the Strait of Bosporus, and the Black Sea on the north. It is an area which comprises most of modern day Turkey. I will suggest that for purposes of "dog talk" either the term Anatolian or the term Turkish is perfectly adequate; so we may as well stay with Anatolian, as it is more commonly used in reference to these dogs.

Confusing enough when we ask questions about where these dogs are from, the confusion greatly intensifies when we ask "exactly what dogs are we referring to?" The argument is essentially between two headstrong factions. We may refer to faction "A" as the unitary faction and to faction "B" as the separatists. The unitary faction feels that the Anatolian Shepherd Dog is that breed of dog found throughout

An Anatolian offers sound conformation and temperament. Photo by Isabelle Français. Owner, Sarah Avery.

Turkey and known as *Çoban Kopegi* or "Shepherd Dog." These enthusiasts describe the color variations of the breed as being buff or white, tricolored, and even black. They feel that, besides the coat color of the dogs, the breed is quite homogeneous; and the fact of the coat colors varying is irrelevant.

The separatists feel that the dogs casually referred to as Anatolian Shepherds are actually two distinct breeds from two district areas of Turkey. Among themselves, the separatists are undecided as to what one of them should be called. They are, however, agreed that one of the two should be called the Akbash Dog.

In Turkey, *Akbash* means white-headed. The Akbash Dog is then that Turkish dog that our unitary faction would call the pure-white Anatolian

Shepherd. Whereas the unitary faction says that, other than the white coloring, the Akbash is identical to all other Anatolian Shepherd Dogs, the separatists tell us that the Akbash is a much more gracefully built animal than the other, heavier boned dogs of Turkey.

The other breed that the separatists tell us is mistakenly confused with the Akbash by the unitary faction is the *Karabash*, or black-headed dog As the name suggests, a typical picture of a Karabash shows a deep black mask. The unitary faction feels that the mask is irrelevant and again, other than coloring, the Akbash and Karabash are the same. As you may have guessed, the separatists feel that the two are very different. Essentially, they tell us that the Karabash is a much heavier bodied and heavier boned dog which clearly displays mastiff ancestry. They show us pictures of very gracefully built white dogs and contrast them with pictures of very heavily

Anatolians wearing traditional collars accompanied by a Turkish shepherd in their native land. The kind of photograph that goes to the heart of the breed and makes a person want to own an Anatolian. Photo by N. Czartoryska.

built black-masked dogs, while the unitary faction tells us that this contrast is nothing more than intentional deception and offers photographs of white and buff dogs standing together that are identical.

Still more confusion exists in the positive identification of these dogs. Among the separatists, someone must have noticed that there are colored dogs that do not have black heads; therefore, the breed name Karabash is not very useful. Upon this realization,

the name Karabash was dropped (although it is still in use among some) and the name Kangal Dog was adopted to refer to the other-than-white Anatolian Shepherds (whether or not the dog in question has a black mask). Those who prefer to employ the designation Kangal Dog to refer to the dark-colored Anatolians (or Karabash Dog, as the case may be) point to what they perceive to be a geographical as well as a typological distinction which in their minds separates the Akbash Dogs from the Kangal Dogs. They tell us that the center of distribution of the Kangal Dog is the Kangal district near Sivas, Turkey, while the Akbash Dog originates just south and west of Ankara.

In brief then, this section might have been headed "The Akbash Dog and the Karabash Dog" or it might have been headed "The Kangal Dog and the Akbash Dog." The fact that I have headed the chapter "The Anatolian Shepherd Dog" should not be misinterpreted as my having taken a firm position in this debate. I employed this breed name purely because it is my belief that many more people know these dogs as Anatolians rather than Akbash, Karabash, or Kangal Dogs. As a means of closing my door in the face of this disagreement, however, I would like to offer the information to any of my readers (who are still interested) that the Kennel Club of England was going through this

The designation "Anatolian Shepherd" has been chosen by the author because it is the most recognizable name for the Turkish shepherd dogs; Anatolian, Karabash, Akbash and Kangal Dogs are all herded together under this nomenclature.

THE ANATOLIAN SHEPHERD DOG

Above: **Hissar Hamsin, a stately Anatolian and a good dog.**
Below: **A fine Anatolian Shepherd Dog keeping watchful guard over the premises. Owner, L. Emanuel. Photo by Isabelle Francais.**

debate for years and at its meeting of May 31, 1983, decided the following: " . . . the breed known hitherto as the Anatolian (Karabash) Dog should be renamed the Anatolian Shepherd Dog . . . ." It also concluded that the color clause in the breed's standard should be altered to permit dogs to be exhibited irrespective of color. The geneticist, Dr. Malcolm Willis, who, along with Dr. Roy Robinson, offered the opinions which figured so heavily in this decision, was later quoted as saying that the unfortunate introduction of the terms "Karabash" and "Akbash" were most regrettable and that he recommended that this terminology be dropped.

Once again, it is my feeling that the low level to which this disagreement has sunk, particularly due to the obvious insecurity of one of the two factions involved, is regrettable in and of itself. I would advise anyone, from either side, who feels motivated to treat this issue as if it were a matter of global importance to step aside and give up the dog fancy, as it has been clearly proven to me that you are doing the popularity of these dogs much more harm than good.

In any event, those among you who don't care to pursue such an in-depth analysis of such trivia but rather are interested in these dogs as suitable companions and effective protection dogs need not become disaffected by the

Anatolian Shepherds. The current lack of popularity of the Anatolians among show enthusiasts, combined with the fact that the breed still depends upon its native Turkey for its functional ability, has allowed these dogs to retain the very authentic temperamental qualities which suit them so well for guard work.

The Anatolian Shepherd is a very large and powerful dog which ranks among the very best of purebred guard dogs today. These dogs develop naturally as protectors of the home and family. In choosing an Anatolian Shepherd puppy as the future guard dog for you, you are absolutely minimizing the chances that your pup will mature to have no interest in guard work. They are among the most willing of canine guardians, and they possess a very high degree of man-

A mock fight between two Anatolians. These Hill Country dogs swim expertly and protect their flock from predatory wolves.

Opposite: A very sturdy-looking Anatolian that would be a joy to own. Owner Henry C. Schley stands proudly over his fine dog. *Below:* These dogs are very gentle with their charges.

stopping ability. As such, it is high time that purebred enthusiasts took a serious look at the Anatolian Shepherd.

The ancestry of the *Coban Kopegi* (Shepherd Dog) of Turkey can be traced to the large and ancient big game hunting and war dogs of Asia Minor and to the guardian breeds of the Ottoman Empire (which lasted about 600 years, until the early part of the 20th century). In the writings of Evliya Efendi (1614–1682), we find reference to the "Samson Dogs," which Evliya says are large, like lions. He also mentions dogs as large as asses and as fierce as lions, and he

goes on to say that on festive days these dogs would be dressed in satin cloth covers and silver collars with iron spikes. During times of peace, the dogs were used to guard livestock, but, during times of war, they were used as dogs of war. In reference to this, Evliya says that one of these dogs would attack a horseman upon command from its master and pull him down from his horse, no matter how stout he might be.

Today's Anatolians are admirably loyal to their masters and fiercely aggressive to intruders. They are very large, very powerful and fearless. As

such, they are used today as guardians and protectors of livestock in Turkey. They are both willing and able to protect the flocks from the predatory animals that still roam this area in search of an easy kill. In fact, the spiked collar sometimes seen on these dogs in Turkey is generally reserved for use on a dog that has proven its worth by actually killing a wolf "singlehandedly."

In spite of the great size of these dogs (100–150 pounds and 29 inches at the withers), they are known to excel as house dogs and pets. This is due to the fact that they tend to be low keyed by nature, generally clean, and lack a strong "doggy" odor. They love to be outdoors as well as indoors, and they are very tolerant of extremes in weather. They tend to be very loyal to their human family, tolerant of children, and suspicious of strangers, but like most of the guardian breeds, generally not good around strange adult dogs. If you live the kind of lifestyle in which you constantly have different people coming in and out of your home, you will likely have trouble raising any guard dog successfully; but in such a situation, even among the

The Akbash Dog. One way or another, it's a handsome dog.

guardian breeds, you would do well to avoid owning any of the Anatolian Shepherds. These dogs typically do not accept anyone but family as fully trusted friends.

How we in the dog fancy have ignored the Anatolian Shepherds to the extent that we have I don't know, but at least until the show scene takes its toll on the character of these dogs, one can do no better than to look among the Anatolian Shepherds for a wonderful family dog and a great man-stopping guard dog.

Standard for the Anatolian Shepherd Dog

GENERAL DESCRIPTION—The Anatolian Shepherd Dog is a large, rugged, powerful and impressive dog possessing great endurance and agility. Forged through a set of very demanding circumstances for a purely utilitarian purpose, he is the working guard dog without equal. The Anatolian is the primary working dog of Asia Minor, used for his ability to protect livestock. The breed has been known under the name Çomar. The accepted modern Turkish name, as it appears on the Government post stamp is Çoban Kopeği which literally means "shepherd dog."

CHARACTER—Being a true livestock protector, the Anatolian Shepherd Dog's deportment is normally alert and intelligent, calm and observant. Instinctively protective, he is extremely protective and highly adaptable to specialized training. He is very loyal and responsive to his master while he is aloof with strangers. Highly territorial, he is a natural guard and, if properly reared, not given to roaming.

HEAD—The skull is large but in proportion to the body. There is a slight centerline furrow, fore and aft, from apparent stop to moderately noticeable occiput. The skull is broader in dogs than bitches.

Eyes—The eyes are medium size and set apart for good depth perception. The worthy dog has excellent visual acuity for day or night surveillance and pursuit. Eye rims should be black and almond shaped without sag or looseness of haw. Eye color ranges from dark brown to light amber.

Ears—The ears are of triangular shape, rounded apex, measuring about 4 inches at the base by about 6 inches in length. The tip of the ear should be just long enough to reach the inside corner of the eyelids. Cropping of ears is

" . . . one can do no better than to look among the Anatolian Shepherds for a wonderful family dog and a great man-stopping guard dog."

common in Turkey.

Mouth and Muzzle—The dog should have a black nose and flews. Flews are normally dry but pronounced enough to contribute to "squaring" the overall muzzle appearance. The muzzle is blockier and stronger for the dog, but neither dogs nor bitches could be described as having a snipey head or muzzle. The dog should have healthy gums and a full complement of strong, healthy teeth with a proper scissor bite.

NECK—The neck should be slightly arched, powerful and muscular, moderate length with more skin and fur than elsewhere on the body, forming a protective ruff. The dewlap should not be pendulous and excessive.

BODY—The body is well proportioned, obviously functional without exaggeration. An Anatolian's muscularity is evident even at rest. He should never be fat or soft. A deep chest and well-sprung rib cage provide the necessary heart and lung room. The distinct tuckup at the loins gives the dog uncommon ability for a dog his size. A powerful, muscular level back without roach or sag, slopes downward at the croup. All in all, proportions combine for great strength and exceptional speed and endurance.

Forequarters—The forelegs should be relatively long, well boned and set straight with strong pasterns. Shoulders should be large, muscular and well developed, blades long, broad and sloping. Elbows should be neither in nor out.

Hindquarters—The hindquarters are strong enough for agile and powerful maneuvering. Thighs are broad and heavily muscled. Angulation at the stifle and hock are in proportion to the forequarters as balance is of utmost importance. As seen from behind, the legs should be parallel to each other.

Feet—The feet are strong and compact with well-arched toes. They should have stout nails with pads thick and tough.

TAIL—The tail should be long and reaching at least to the hocks. It is set rather high. When relaxed it is carried low with the end curved upwards. When alert, the tail is carried high, some making a "wheel."

GAIT—At the trot, the gait is powerful yet fluid and well coordinated. When viewed from the front or rear, the legs turn neither in nor out, nor do feet cross nor interfere with each other. With increased speed, footfall converges towards the centerline of gravity. When viewed from the side, the

front legs should reach out smoothly with no obvious pounding. The withers and backline should stay nearly level with little rise or fall. The rear assembly should push out smoothly with hocks doing their share of the work and flexing well, showing power and strength.

COAT—Variations in length and texture are acceptable, from the short straight coat to the longer, slightly wavy one. The coat is somewhat longer and thicker at the neck and mane. A thick undercoat is common to all, feathering normal, and proportional to coat length. Matted, curly, or corded coat is not acceptable.

SIZE (AGE 2 OR OLDER)—Weight: Dogs from 100 pounds. Bitches from 80 pounds. Size: Dogs from 29 inches. Bitches from 27 inches.

Minimums do not apply to individuals less than 2 years of age. While larger size is attractive, it should not take precedence over correct breed type, soundness, balance, and temperament.

Faults—Any deviation from the aforementioned specifications is a fault. The degree to which a dog is penalized depends on the extent to which the dog deviates from the standard and the extent to which the particular fault would actually affect the working ability of the dog.

The Akbash Dog is solid white with somewhat extensive feathering; some believe that these dogs appear to be more leggy than the Anatolians. Owner, Dee Gannon.

THE BOUVIER DES FLANDRES

Opposite: **The Bouvier des Flandres is a great companion dog who really looks the part of man's best friend. Owner, Alex Saunders.** *Left:* **Two dirty-bearded Bouviers head-to-head. Owner, Van Vliet Kennel.**

I clearly remember the first time I ever saw a Bull Terrier, and the first time I ever saw a Giant Schnauzer. It was fortunate for my general experience with purebreds that my first experience with these breeds was with exceptional individuals (or so my memory tells me), and I was terrifically impressed by each. The first time I ever saw an American Pit Bull Terrier, an eight-month-old, pure-white male out of excellent lines, I dug into my wallet and bought the dog on the spot. I owned him for many years. I also clearly recall the circumstances under which I saw my first Bouvier. I was in my early teens at the time and didn't carry money with me. Had I been a grown man, I'm sure the owner would have gotten an offer for his dog that day.

I remember that it was a cool, breezy fall day. I was walking around a lake in New York City looking into the

91

water through the fallen red and brown oak leaves floating on the surface, in search of whatever aquatic wildlife might care to give me a private viewing. There weren't many people around. As I walked looking into the water, the last thing I expected to hear was a deep, steady, very serious growl. I turned and would have sworn that I was staring into the face of the Werewolf of London. The dog was seated and attached by a leash to a friendly looking man who smiled and told me that the dog was completely secure and really just warning me of his presence. Still, looking into that shaggy face with its utterly fearless expression, I asked the owner what kind of dog it was and learned that it was a Bouvier. I committed the name to memory for future reference.

Years later I had the opportunity to live and work in the Netherlands for awhile, and this was where I became more familiar with the Bouvier. In Holland and Belgium, one commonly sees Bouvier dogs. There the dog is known not only for its striking appearance but also for its abilities as a working dog and especially as a willing and powerful guardian breed. I may not be the right person to ask about the

usefulness of the Bouvier as a deterrent against crime, because when I look at one of these dogs, I still see the Werewolf of London. A good Bouvier could deter me from walking into my own house, let alone anyone else's.

The Bouvier can grow to be a fairly tall dog (as much as 27½ inches at the withers for a large male), but it is not an exceptionally big dog. Its thick, dense coat and its muscular body aid in giving the Bouvier a very large, bear-like (or werewolf-like) appearance. It is a beautiful dog in a somewhat aristocratic sort of way, which is something of an irony considering the shepherding ancestry of the breed.

Frankly, the Bouvier is one of today's purebreds which in its current show form has, in my opinion, no really meaningful history. Historically, the ancestors of the modern Bouvier were among the general sheepdogs of Belgium which, though functionally very useful, were of no specific size or physical type.

It was not until the 1890 s, when Professor Reul of the Veterinary School of Brussels drew attention to a few general physical types of sheepdogs then existing in Belgium, that breeders began focusing specifically on some of these types. One type went on to become today's Bouvier. This type, however, was very different in appearance from the beautiful show specimens available today.

It is a credit to Belgian breeders that such a fine physical type was fixed without costing the breed its functional ability. This is largely due to the fact that, in Belgium, a dog must prove its abilities as a police, defense, or army dog in order to attain the title "Champion." The breed owes its development as a show dog primarily to a written standard adopted in 1912.

The Bouvier breed took a

Two very good-looking Bouviers. Photo by Isabelle Français. Owner, Van Vliet Kennel.

serious blow to its progress during World War I, when most of Belgium's Bouviers either died or were taken by the Germans. A few owners did manage to keep their dogs throughout the war, and from these dogs the breed continued to develop.

The Bouvier is a great all-around breed for anyone who wants a good guard dog. It is powerful, fearless, determined, and suitable as a useful man-stopper. On the other hand, the breed generally is of such a steady disposition that it is often used as a guide dog for the blind in Europe. It is known as an excellent family dog and as a breed which is normally very tolerant of children. It is comfortable as an outdoor or an indoor dog and is of suitable size to keep in the home. If you find that the physical type of the Bouvier appeals to you, I would not hesitate to depend upon one as a home guardian of great capability. The breed is readily available, and the quality of the Bouviers produced is generally excellent.

The Bouvier is a very popular breed in Europe and it exists in beautiful form in the U.S. as well, thanks to careful judging. Photo by Isabelle Français. Owner, Renee Berand.

Standard for the Bouvier des Flandres

GENERAL DESCRIPTION—The Bouvier des Flandres is a powerfully built, compact, short-coupled, rough-coated dog of notably rugged appearance. He gives the depicting his intelligence, vigor and daring. By nature he is an equable dog.

His origin is that of a cattle herder and a general farmer's helper, including cart pulling. He is an ideal farm dog. His harsh coat protects him in all weather, enabling him to perform the most arduous tasks. The coat may

A fine Bouvier. Photo by Isabelle Français. Owner, Van Vliet Kennel.

impression of great strength without any sign of heaviness or clumsiness in his overall makeup. He is agile, spirited and bold, yet his serene, well-behaved disposition denotes his steady, resolute and fearless character. His gaze is alert and brilliant, be trimmed slightly only to accent the body line. Overtrimming which alters the natural rugged appearance is to be avoided. He has been used as an ambulance and messenger dog. Modern times find him as a watch and guard dog as well as family friend, guardian and protector. His physical and mental characteristics and deportment, coupled with his olfactory abilities, his intelligence and initiative, enable him also to perform as a tracking dog and a guide dog for the blind.

HEAD—The head is impressive in scale, accentuated by beard and mustache. It is in proportion to body and build.

Skull—Well developed and flat, slightly less wide than long. When viewed from the side, the top lines of the skull and the muzzle are parallel. It is wide between the ears, with the frontal groove barely marked. The stop is more apparent than real, due to upstanding eyebrows. The proportions of length of skull to length of muzzle are 3 to 2.

Eyes—The expression is bold and alert. They neither protrude nor are sunken in the sockets. Their shape is oval with the axis on a horizontal plane, when viewed from

A serious guardian as well as a good friend. Photo by Isabelle Français. Owner, Renee Berand.

Pulling the milk cart was an important part of Bouvier history. Photo by Isabelle Français. Owner, Van Vliet Kennel.

the front. Their color is dark nut brown. The eye rims are black without lack of pigment and the haw is barely visible. Yellow or light eyes are to be strongly penalized, along with a wall-eyed or staring expression.

Ears—Placed high and alert. They are rough-coated. If cropped, they are to be a triangular contour and in proportion to the size of the head. The inner corner of the ear should be in line with the outer corner of the eye. Ears that are too low or too closely set are serious faults.

Muzzle—Broad, strong, well filled out, tapering gradually toward the nose without ever becoming snipy or pointed. The cheeks are flat and lean, with the lips being dry and tight fitting. A narrow, snipy muzzle is faulty.

Nose—Large, black, well developed, round at the edges, with flared nostrils. A brown, pink or spotted nose is a serious fault.

Jaws and Teeth—The jaws are powerful and of equal length. The teeth are strong, white and healthy, with the incisors meeting in a scissors bite. Overshot or undershot bites are to be severely penalized.

NECK—The neck is strong and muscular, widening gradually into the shoulders. When viewed from the side, it is gracefully arched with upright carriage. A short, squatty neck is faulty. No dewlap.

BODY OR TRUNK—
Powerful, broad and short. The length from the point of the shoulder to the tip of the buttocks is equal to the height from the ground to the highest point of the withers. The chest is broad, with the brisket extending to the elbow in depth. A long-lined, rangy dog should be faulted.

Ribs—The ribs are deep and well sprung. The first ribs are slightly curved, the others well sprung and very sloped nearing the rear, giving proper depth to the chest. Flat ribs or slabsidedness to be strongly penalized.

Back—Short, broad, well muscled with firm level topline. It is supple and flexible with no sign of weakness.

Flanks and Loins—Short, wide and well muscled, without weakness. The abdomen is only slightly tucked up.

Croup or Rump—The horizontal line of the back should mold unnoticeably into the curve of the rump, which is characteristically wide. A sunken or slanted croup is a serious fault.

Forequarters—Strong boned, well muscled and straight.

Shoulder and upper arms—The shoulders are

Can't you just see how fierce a Bouvier can be when angry? Photo by Robert Pearcy.

The Bouvier is a very obedient, trainable dog who can excel in obedience trials. Photo by Isabelle Français. Owner, Van Vliet Kennel.

relatively long, muscular but not loaded, with good layback. The shoulder blade and humerus are approximately the same length, forming an angle slightly greater than 90 degrees when standing. Straight shoulders are faulty.

Elbows—Close to the body and parallel. Elbows which are too far out or in are faults.

Forearms—Viewed either in profile of from the front are perfectly straight, parallel to each other and perpendicular to the ground. They are well muscled and strong boned.

Wrists—Exactly in line with the forearms. Strong boned.

Pasterns—Quite short, slightly sloped forward. Dewclaws may be removed.

Hindquarters—Firm, well muscled with large, powerful hams. They should be parallel with the front legs when viewed from either front or rear.

Thighs—Wide and muscular. Upper thigh must be neither too straight nor too sloping. There is moderate angulation at the stifle.

Legs—Moderately long, well muscled, neither too straight nor too inclined.

Hocks—Strong, rather

close to the ground. When standing and seen from the rear, they will be straight and perfectly parallel to each other and perpendicular to the ground. In motion, they must turn neither in nor out. There is a slight angulation at the hock joint. Sickle or cow hocks are serious faults.

Metatarsi—Hardy and lean, rather cylindrical and perpendicular to the ground when standing. If born with dewclaws, they are to be removed.

FEET—Both forefeet and hind feet are rounded and compact turning neither in nor out; the toes close and well arched; strong black nails; thick tough pads.

TAIL—Is to be docked, leaving 2 or 3 vertebrae. It must be set high and align normally with the spinal column. Preferably carried upright in motion. Dogs born tailless should not be penalized.

COAT—A tousled, double coat capable of withstanding the hardest work in the most inclement weather. The outer hairs are rough and harsh, with the undercoat being fine, soft and dense.

Topcoat—Must be harsh to the touch, dry, trimmed, if necessary, to a length of approximately 2½ inches. A coat too long or too short is a fault, as is a silky or wooly coat. It is tousled without being curly. On the skull, it is short. On the upper part of the back, it is particularly close and harsh always, however, remaining rough.

Undercoat—A dense mass of fine, close hair, thicker in winter. Together with the top coat, it will form a water-resistant covering. A flat coat, denoting lack of undercoat is a serious fault.

Mustache and Beard—Very thick, with the hair being shorter and rougher on the upper side of the muzzle. The upper lip with its heavy mustache and the chin with its heavy and rough beard give that gruff expression so characteristic of the breed.

Eyebrows—Erect hairs accentuating the shape of the eyes without ever veiling them.

Color—From fawn to black, passing through salt and pepper, gray, and brindle. A small white star on the chest is allowed. Other than chocolate brown, white or parti-color, which is to be severely penalized, no other color is to be favored.

HEIGHT—The height as measured at the withers—Dogs, from 24½ to 27½ inches; bitches from 23½ to 26½ inches. In each sex, the ideal height is the median of the the two limits, i.e., 26 inches for a dog and 25 inches for a bitch. Any dog or bitch deviating from the minimum or maximum limits mentioned shall be severely penalized.

GAIT—The whole of the Bouvier des Flandres must be harmoniously proportioned to allow for a free, bold and proud gait. The reach of the forequarters must compensate for and be in balance with the driving power of the hindquarters. The back, while moving in a trot, will remain firm and flat. In general, the gait is the logical demonstration of the structure and build of the dog. It is to be noted that while moving at a fast trot, the properly built Bouvier will tend to single-track.

TEMPERAMENT—The Bouvier is an equable dog, steady, resolute and fearless. Viciousness or shyness is undesirable.

FAULTS—The foregoing description is that of the ideal Bouvier des Flandres. Any deviation from this is to be penalized to the extent of the deviation.

Wrap it up. I'll take it! If this picture doesn't appeal to you, then you need to select another breed. Owner, Van Vliet Kennel.

THE BOXER

Opposite:
**Although
cropping the
Boxer is
traditional,
natural ears
become the
breed nicely.**

Above: **Young
Boxer pups
belonging to
Rick Tomita.
Photo by
Isabelle
Français.**

In the study of the origin and history of purebred dogs, we find in virtually all instances that it really makes very little sense to try to claim any one country as the sole place of origin for any breed. An interest in a breed is a geographic and cultural pursuit, the contributions toward which rarely begin or end at the border of any one country. The development of the Boxer breed will clearly demonstrate this point.

The Boxer is universally accepted as being a breed of German origin. We know that medium- to large-sized, short-faced dogs with very powerfully constructed bodies were commonly used in the spectator sport of animal baiting throughout much of Western Europe during the sixteenth, seventeenth, and eighteenth centuries. Precisely where these breeds originated and from what basic "component" breeds they were developed remain questions for active discussion. The many types of dogs developed for their participation in animal (especially bull) baits were often referred to by the generic term "bulldog," but each developed regional characteristics which qualified them as distinct breeds.

In addition to their general body style and their incredible gameness, these regionally specific gladiators shared other interesting characteristics. One such characteristic was that each normally came in two sizes, a small size (about 50 pounds) and a large size (more than 80 pounds). The need for two sizes in the view of the animal-baiting fraternity of the day was that whereas a smaller, more agile dog might prove more effective at baiting a bull, a larger, harder hitting dog would stand a better chance against a bear. As bull and bear baits were very common throughout Spain, Portugal, Germany, England, France, Holland, etc., baiting enthusiasts developed their own separate version of both bearbaiters and bullbaiters.

In Germany, two gladiator breeds which were considered to be distinct, primarily due to the size difference between them, were known as the *Bullenbeisser* (bull biter) and the *Barenbeisser* (bear biter). Coincidentally, while the first mention of the Bulldog in England appears in a letter written in 1631, the first mention of the *Bullenbeisser* in Germany appears in writing from 1632. Here the *Bullenbeisser* was distinguished from the *Barenbeisser*. Seventeenth- and even sixteenth-century paintings of these dogs from Germany clearly depict a smaller dog of the general Boxer-type and a larger dog of a very similar type but with more mastiff-like characteristics, especially size.

The bloodlines of all the bull- and bear-baiting dogs were undoubtedly influenced by each other. Not only did all of these dogs probably share very common ancestry but, as Western European bullbaiters were exclusively concerned with functional ability rather than with the maintenance of any particular body type, the crossing of one regional strain with another would have been a simple matter of course and solely dependent upon which strains were performing best at any given time. As a result, it is not surprising that the Bulldogs of England and those of Germany were very similar in appearance and temperament during the long period of their employment for functional purposes.

It is uncertain precisely

when, where, or why the term Boxer came into use in Germany, but it was the German *Bullenbeisser* form that was eventually to be referred to by this name, and today's Boxer is essentially an expression of this type of dog. The Boxer type remained in existence in Germany as well as elsewhere, but modern Boxer lines actually stem from a bitch named "Flora" that was imported to Munich, Germany, from France in 1887 by George Alt. This bitch was bred to a local male, and the inbreeding of the progeny of this line is at the root of all modern Boxer lines.

The great-great-granddaughter of the dog imported from France by George Alt is generally regarded as the mother of the Boxer breed. This is especially interesting when we consider

that this bitch, registered as Meta von der Passage No. 30, was produced by crossing a Boxer bitch of the line which stems from George Alt's French import to a pure-white English Bulldog by the name of "Tom." This breeding produced a pure-white half-Bulldog, half-Boxer bitch by the registry name of Ch. Blanka No. 4, and this bitch became the mother of Meta von der Passage No. 30, the bitch who appears in the early pedigree of all modern Boxers.

The fact that many early Boxers contained a great deal of white in their coats, that one of the earliest Champion Boxers was pure white (not to mention half-Bulldog) and that the English Bulldog, which was often white, played such an important role in early Boxer development, account for the commonality of the occurrence of white Boxers in modern litters. While any more than a one-third white coat is viewed as a serious fault among modern show enthusiasts, the white coloring clearly has its place in Boxer history.

Today's Boxer is as much as one can hope any family dog to be. It is fun-loving, people-loving, and generally a wonderful dog for children. It is a short-haired breed of moderate size, well endowed with both strength and agility. But is it a reliable man-stopping guard dog? The answer to this is both yes and no, depending upon where you get your dog.

Like many of the real powerhouse breeds that have attained a fairly high level of popularity among dog show enthusiasts, the aggressive quality of the Boxer which took breeders of old literally centuries to cultivate has been systematically subdued by modern Boxer breeders. In consideration of the gladiator history of this breed, it is highly ironic to have to offer this word of caution about the breed, but, in fact, to purchase a Boxer at random is to run the high risk of ending up with a dog which will be utterly useless as a guardian.

There are some Boxers that do work well as guardians, and your chance of selecting one of these can be improved by interviewing breeders carefully. I must tell you, however, that if I were in the market for a Boxer that I intended to use as a willing and able man-stopper, I would invest the extra money and effort involved in having a German-bred dog imported. German breeders generally are more interested in the actual proven ability of Boxer bloodlines than most others tend to be. Quality pet dealers will often establish correspondence in Germany for you if you express your interest

Some would say that these Boxers are . . . well, boxing. Photo by Français. Owner, Rick Tomita.

in obtaining such a dog. If you are willing to do this, you stand an excellent chance of choosing a terrific man-stopper from among the Boxer breed. Always be careful whom you are dealing with when you buy any dog sight unseen.

Before dropping this matter, let me point out that the lack of working ability among so many purebreds is a very unfortunate development. Any breeder who invests the necessary energy in producing a physically perfect representative of a breed yet ignores working ability and true breed temperament has really missed the entire point of dog breeding.

Standard for the Boxer

GENERAL APPEARANCE—The Boxer is a medium-sized, sturdy dog, of square build, with short back, strong

limbs, and short, tight-fitting coat. His musculation, well developed, should be clean, hard and appear smooth (not bulging) under taut skin. His movements should denote energy. The gait is firm yet elastic (springy), the stride free and ground-covering, the carriage proud and noble. Developed to serve the multiple purposes of guard, working and escort-dog, he must combine elegance with substance and ample power, not alone for beauty, but to ensure the speed, dexterity and jumping ability essential to arduous hike, riding expedition, police or military duty. Only a body whose individual parts are built to withstand the most strenuous efforts, assembled as a complete and harmonious whole, can respond to these combined demands. Therefore, to be at his highest efficiency he must

A well-muscled, easy-moving American Boxer. I could see myself with a dog like this, I guess. World Dog Show, 1986.

never be plump or heavy, and, while equipped for great speed, he must never be racy.

The head imparts to the Boxer a unique individual stamp, peculiar to him alone. It must be in perfect proportion to his body, never small in comparison to the overall picture. The muzzle is his most distinctive feature, and great value is to be placed on its being of correct form and in absolute proper proportion to the skull.

In judging the Boxer, first consideration should be given to the general appearance; next, overall balance, including the desired proportions of the individual parts of the body to each other, as well as the relation of substance to elegance—to which an attractive color or arresting style may contribute. Special attention is to be devoted to the head, after which the dog's individual components are to be examined for the correct construction and function, and efficiency of gait evaluated. **Faults**—Head not typical, plump bulldoggy appearance, light bone, lack of balance, bad condition, lack of noble bearing.

HEAD—The beauty of the head depends upon the harmonious proportion of the muzzle to the skull. The muzzle should always appear powerful, never small in its relationship to the skull. The head should be clean, not showing deep wrinkles. Folds will normally appear upon the forehead when the ears are erect, and they are always indicated from the lower edge of the stop running downward on both sides of the muzzle. The dark mask is confined to the muzzle and is in direct

A brindle Boxer.

contrast to the color of the head. Any extension of the mask to the skull, other than dark shading around the eyes, creates a somber, undesirable expression. When white replaces any of the black mask, the path of any upward extension should be between the eyes. The muzzle is powerfully developed in length, width and depth. It is not pointed, narrow, short or shallow. Its shape is influenced first through the formation of both jawbones, second through the placement of teeth, and third through the texture of the lips.

The Boxer is normally undershot. Therefore, the lower jaw protrudes beyond the upper and curves slightly upward. The upper jaw is broad where attached to the skull and maintains this breadth except for a very slight tapering to the front. The incisor teeth of the lower jaw are in a straight line, the canines preferably up front in the same line to give the jaw the greatest possible width. The line of incisors in the upper jaw is slightly convex toward the front. The upper corner incisors should fit snugly back of the lower canine teeth on each side, reflecting the symmetry essential to the creation of a sound, non-slip bite.

The lips which complete the formation of the muzzle should meet evenly. The upper lip is thick and padded, filling out the frontal space created by the projection of the lower jaw. It rests on the edge of the lower lip and, laterally, is supported by the fangs (canines) of the lower jaw. Therefore, these fangs must stand far apart, and be of good length so that the front surface of the muzzle is broad and squarish and, when viewed from the side, forms an obtuse angle with the topline of the muzzle. Over-protrusion of the overlip or underlip is undesirable. The chin should be perceptible when viewed from the side as well as from the front without being over-repandous (rising above the bite line) as in the Bulldog. The Boxer must not show teeth or tongue when the mouth is closed. Excessive flews are not desirable. The top of the skull is slightly arched, not rotund, flat, nor noticeably broad, and the occiput not too pronounced. The forehead forms a distinct stop with the

A cropped Boxer pup with adhesive-supported ears. In Europe, the Boxer is not cropped. Photographed by Vince Serbin.

Musculature and dignity combine to distinguish Tomita Boxers. Photo by Français.

topline of the muzzle, which must not be forced back into the forehead like that of a Bulldog. It should not slant down (down-faced), nor should it be dished, although the tip of the nose should lie somewhat higher than the root of the muzzle. The forehead shows just a slight furrow between the eyes. The cheeks, although covering powerful masseter muscles compatible with the strong set of teeth, should be relatively flat and not bulge, maintaining the clean lines of the skull. They taper into the muzzle in a slight, graceful curve. The ears are set at the highest points of the sides of the skull, cut rather long without too broad a shell, and are carried erect. The dark brown eyes, not too small, protruding or deep-set, are encircled by dark hair, and should impart an alert, intelligent expression. Their mood-mirroring quality combined with the mobile skin furrowing of the forehead gives the Boxer head its unique degree of expressiveness. The nose is broad and black, very slightly turned up; the nostrils broad, with the nasolabial line running between them down through the upper lip, which, however, must not be split. **Faults**—Lack of nobility and expression, somber face, unserviceable bite. Pinscher or Bulldog head, sloping topline of muzzle, muzzle too light for skull, too pointed a bite (snipy). Teeth or tongue showing with mouth closed, driveling, split upper lip. Poor ear carriage, light "Bird of Prey" eyes.

NECK—Round, of ample length, not too short; strong, muscular and clean throughout, without dewlap; distinctly marked nape with an elegant arch running down to the back. **Fault**—Dewlap.

BODY—In profile, the build is of square proportions in that a horizontal line from the front of the forechest to the rear projection of the upper thigh should equal a vertical line dropped from the top of the withers to the ground.

Chest and Forequarters—The brisket is deep, reaching down to the elbows; the depth of the body at the lowest point of the brisket equals half the height of the dog at the withers. The ribs, extending far to the rear, are well arched but not barrel-shaped. Chest of fair width and forechest well defined, being easily visible from the side. The loins are short and muscular; the lower stomach line, lightly tucked up, blends into a graceful curve to the rear. The shoulders are long and sloping, close-lying and not excessively covered with muscle. The upper arm is long, closely approaching a right angle to the shoulder blade. The forelegs, viewed from the front, are straight, stand parallel to each other, and have strong, firmly joined bones. The elbows should not press too closely to the chest wall or stand off visibly from it. The forearm is straight, long and firmly muscled. The pastern joint is clearly defined but not distended. The pastern is strong and distinct, slightly slanting, but standing almost perpendicular to the ground. The dewclaws may be removed as a safety precaution. Feet should be compact, turning neither in nor out, with tightly arched toes (cat feet) and tough pads. **Faults**—Chest too broad, too shallow or too deep in front; loose or overmuscled shoulders; chest hanging between the shoulders; tied-in or bowed-out elbows; turned feet; hare feet; hollow flanks; hanging stomach.

Back—The withers should be clearly defined as the highest point of the back; the whole back short,

A good Boxer promises to be a reliable watchdog and protector.

straight and muscular with a firm topline. **Faults**— Roach back, sway back, thin lean back, long narrow loins, weak union with croup.

Hindquarters—Strongly muscled with angulation in balance with that of forequarters. The thighs broad and curved, the breech musculature hard and strongly developed. Croup slightly sloped, flat and broad. Tail attachment high rather than low. Tail clipped, carried upward. Pelvis long and, in females especially, broad. Upper and lower thigh long, leg well angulated with a clearly defined, well-let-down hock joint. In standing position, the leg below the hock joint (metatarsus) should be practically perpendicular to the ground, with a slight rearward slope permissible. Viewed from behind, the hindlegs should be straight, with the hock joints leaning neither in nor out. The metatarsus should be short, clean and strong, supported by powerful rear pads. The rear toes just a little longer than the front toes, but similar in all other respects. Dewclaws, if any, may be removed. **Faults**—Too rounded, too narrow, or falling off of croup; low-set tail; higher in back than in front; steep, stiff, or too slightly angulated hindquarters; light thighs; bowed or crooked legs; cowhocks; overangulated hock joints (sickle hocks);

The Boxer's success in the show ring cannot be denied. In America and Europe, the breed remains popular and dependable. This is Ch. Cher Kei's Son-Of-A-Gun, owned by Cheryl and Keith Robbins. Photo by Robert Forsyth.

long metatarsus (high hocks); hare feet; hindquarters too far under or too far behind.

GAIT—Viewed from the side, proper front and rear angulation is manifested in a smoothly efficient, level-backed, ground covering stride with powerful drive emanating from a freely operating rear. Although the front legs do not contribute impelling power, adequate "reach" should be evident to prevent interference, overlap or "side-winding" (crabbing). Viewed from the front, the shoulders should remain trim and the elbows not flare out. The legs are parallel until gaiting narrows the track in proportion to increasing speed, then the legs come in under the body but should never cross. The line from the shoulder down through the leg should remain straight, although not necessarily perpendicular to the ground. Viewed from the rear, a Boxer's breech should not roll. The hind feet should "dig in" and track relatively true with the front. Again, as speed increases, the normally broad rear track will become narrower. **Faults**—Stilted or inefficient gait, pounding, paddling or flailing out of front legs, rolling or waddling gait, tottering hock joints, crossing over or interference—front or rear, lack of smoothness.

HEIGHT—Adult males— 22½ to 25 inches; females— 21 to 23½ inches at the withers. Males should not go under the minimum nor females over the maximum.

COAT—Short, shiny, lying smooth and tight to the body.

Color—The colors are fawn and brindle. Fawn in various shades from light tan to stag red or mahogany, the deeper colors preferred. The brindle coat in the Boxer is of two opposite types. The first of these includes those dogs having clearly defined dark stripes on a fawn background. The second type has what is best termed reverse brindling. Here the effect is of a very dark background with lighter colored fawn stripes or streaks showing through. White markings on fawn or brindle dogs are not to be rejected and are often very attractive, but must be limited to one-third of the ground color and are not desirable on the back of the torso proper. On the face, white may replace a part or all of the otherwise essential black mask. However, these markings should be ot such distribution as to enhance and not detract from true Boxer expression.

CHARACTER AND TEMPERAMENT— These are of paramount importance in the Boxer. Instinctively a "hearing"

guard dog, his bearing is alert, dignified and self assured, even at rest. In the show ring, his behavior should exhibit constrained animation. With family and friends, his temperament is fundamentally playful, yet patient and stoical with children. Deliberate and wary with strangers, he will exhibit curiosity, but, most importantly, fearless courage and tenacity if threatened.

However, he responds promptly to friendly overtures when honestly rendered. His intelligence, loyal affection and tractability to discipline make him a highly desirable companion. **Faults**—Lack of dignity and alertness, shyness, cowardice, treachery and viciousness (belligerency towards other dogs should not be considered viciousness).

THE BULLMASTIFF

Opposite: **A fiery-eyed and intense candidate for guard duty. Owner, E. Elitz.** *Left:* **A pretty serious-looking Bullmastiff. I'll say this: make one of these dogs mad and there's no stopping it. This is Ch. Favodemil Calif of Baghdad, owned by Vic Zeoli.**

There are hundreds of breeds of purebred dogs in existence throughout the world today, most of which were developed to serve man in one specific fashion or another. Of them, very few were developed by man for the purpose of attacking man. The Bullmastiff is one of these very few breeds.

As its breed name implies, the Bullmastiff was originally created by crossing the Mastiff of England to the once functionally capable and highly spirited Bulldog. Before proceeding here, it is imperative that we not envision the breed as being simply a cross between the modern show representatives of these component breeds. A cross between the modern-day Mastiff and the modern-day, functionally useless, Bulldog would undoubtedly produce a similarly useless animal that would have been of no interest to those who created the original Bullmastiff of England.

The bull-and-mastiff cross was an idea hardly unique to those who developed the dogs that gave rise to today's breed. Even today, the intentional crossbreeding of such purebreds as the Neapolitan Mastiff and the American Pit Bull Terrier is common—such crosses often produce wonderfully loyal, very willing and able guard dogs.

Many of the breeds discussed in this book are essentially the product of a bull-and-mastiff cross. Early reference to bull-and-mastiff dogs appears in French literature long before our modern-day Bullmastiff came into being. As such, the nineteenth-century British breeding experiments that ultimately produced the forerunners of this modern purebred were really just one of many phases of experiments. Fortunately for modern Bullmastiff enthusiasts, this experiment was the beginning of a long-range program that eventually fixed a purebred type.

Today's purebred Bullmastiff owes its origin to a situation that developed about the middle of the nineteenth century in England. At that time, owners of large estates were being victimized by

poachers who would sneak onto the estates at night and poach game. Penalties for poaching were very severe but did not deter the poachers. Instead, these penalties often had the negative effect of prompting poachers to remain uncaught at all cost. Gamekeepers, in pursuit of poachers, began to find themselves in serious, life-threatening situations when they caught up with these intruders; therefore, they came upon the idea of developing the ultimate "gamekeeper's night dog" for their own protection. Early experiments involved crossing many of the most powerful breeds of the time, such as the Bulldog, the Wolfhound, the German Mastiff (Great Dane), etc., but it was the cross between the Bulldog and the Mastiff that was eventually found to be most effective.

Early gamekeepers were not concerned with the development of purebred lines; rather, they were concerned only with a dog's functional ability. The bull-and-mastiff cross that originally defined the Bullmastiff was typically a 50/50 cross. Later, a breeder by the name of S.S. Mosely, considered today as the originator of the modern Bullmastiff breed, crossed mastiffs and bulldogs in proportions of 60% to 40% respectively.

Mosely fixed his type to demonstrate these proportions. This began a debate among Bullmastiff fanciers and historians that remains alive and well today and will probably never be fully resolved to everyone's satisfaction. When one hears a Bullmastiff fancier express a preference for a "bully" dog, while another stands his ground on his preference for a bigger, more "mastiffy" type, each can be correct and support his claim with solid historical evidence. You can resolve this debate in your own mind by deciding which appearance you happen to prefer and adopting a case that will support your selection. Personally, I prefer a smaller (110 to 125 pound) "bully" dog, so I argue in favor of the gamekeepers. If you prefer a more mastiff-like dog, you may fly the Mosely flag. In general, British breeders prefer a 50/50 dog while American breeders prefer a 60/40 dog.

In any event, the combination of the large and

A handsome and appealing Bullmastiff.

powerful Mastiff and the fast, powerful, and courageous Bulldog proved to be a very capable animal. Its functional ability was proven not only on the job but also in field trials in which a muzzled Bullmastiff was to overtake, bring down, and hold a 200-pound man on the run. The man would be given a head start and often a club to defend himself, but it was always clearly demonstrated that no man was a match for a Bullmastiff.

History tells us that the Bullmastiff was never intended to be a mauler. Instead, it is said that the dog's job was to find, catch, bring down, and detain a poacher so that the man could be brought to justice. Many fanciers of early bull-and-mastiff breed crosses are somewhat skeptical about

the fate of most poachers caught by the old gamekeeper's night dog. In any case, considering that a poacher who was caught could very well be facing the death penalty for his crime, one can only imagine the terrific fights for freedom and survival that must have taken place when the Bullmastiff of old came upon his opponent in the night.

As the Bullmastiff was used as a night-dog in the early days of the breed, it was the dark-colored dogs that were preferred. The black brindle dogs particularly were favored. Brindle Bullmastiffs still exist in great numbers and are shown in show rings, but their popularity has given way to the much more popular fawn-colored dogs. I see this as being an unfortunate development,

A powerful-looking Bullmastiff that really displays the physical characteristics of both the Bulldog and the Mastiff.

Simon and Flora Slater with their Bullmastiff Rocky. Rocky was 130 pounds the last time I saw him; that was some time ago.

and I would urge anyone in the market for a Bullmastiff to consider the brindle dog first. Always choose a sound dog, however; such characteristics as color should only be taken into consideration after a selection of sound dogs has been located.

As an aside, I found myself in precisely this position only a few years ago. I was in the market for a Bullmastiff pup to raise with my young sons. I am especially partial to brindle Bullmastiffs. I like a deep red coat color almost as much, and I don't particularly care for a fawn-coated dog. I ended up selecting a fawn dog because none of the brindles or reds then available looked as sound as I would have preferred.

The best breeding stock available today seems to be found in the U.S.A. However, I personally have serious concern for the process of selection employed by modern Bullmastiff breeders—and with the resulting quality of today's Bullmastiff stock. In fact, I am so unhappy with the breed and its breeders on the whole that I'd like to relate my experience with this breed to you.

I have purchased, either for myself or for friends, five Bullmastiff puppies, all from top show breeders and top show lines (and carrying very high price tags too, I should add). The first was a pup I purchased for myself as a family dog. The remaining four were for friends who had met my dog, liked him and asked me to find good Bullmastiffs for them. I bred my dog at ten months of age to a similarly well-bred bitch. Two pups were produced. Including these two pups, this story is now about seven Bullmastiffs—all of whom were family dogs and received excellent care and abounding love.

THE BULLMASTIFF

To make a long story short, consider the following: My Bullmastiff was apparently born with a defective immune system. For three years and four months I battled one infection after another, from bleeding sores that covered his

basement and refused to come out of his kennel, we were forced to make the decision to have him put down.

Of the two puppies born of the breeding we conducted, one died of "natural" causes at eight months of age. By

I took this picture in Virginia and I have to tell you that I really admired this Bullmastiff. Doesn't he look like "the Gamekeeper's Night Dog"?

face for the first year and a half of his life—and which ended his life—to interdigital cysts, enormous skin infections occurring every few months, to constant ear infections and incurable eye infections that ultimately led to his blindness at age three. When the blind dog finally retired to our

natural, I do not mean he was hit by a truck; I mean he was born with a health problem that killed him in eight months. I lost track of the other pup, so I don't know what its physical condition is. The last I heard it was in good shape.

Of the four pups I purchased for friends, one had a kidney

disorder. He went into shock and was euthanized near death at five months of age. The dog's owners were given a new puppy by the breeder of the first dog and it turned out to be a healthy animal.

Of the two remaining pups I purchased, one is healthy in all respects except that he has the weakest stomach I have ever come across in the world of dogs. The dog's owner (who grew up in a family that raised for show Bulldogs and Bull Terriers) swears that even a single pea will set off this 125-pound dog's stomach.

Finally, the last Bullmastiff I purchased for a friend is now over two years of age. He is a 140-pound monster and a picture of absolute good health. My friends are so happy with the dog that they are currently in search of another Bullmastiff. I certainly hope their dog continues to enjoy its good health for at least another six years or so, as even a healthy Bullmastiff is only expected to last eight years or so—and the larger males are lucky to make that.

As far as I am concerned, if my experience with this breed typifies what one can expect of the Bullmastiff, these dogs are most unrecommended as companion dogs and as guard dogs. If the point of perfecting a line of purebreds is to win

The Bullmastiff is an inquiring and tough dog. Photograph by Isabelle Français.

shows by keeping a kennel full of dogs and showing those that are physically able to climb into the ring and look good for awhile, then I suppose my objection to this breed is an unfair one.

If, on the other hand, the point of buying a dog is to share your home and to a large extent your life with a canine companion, I would advise you to select any breed but this one. If the point is to have an effective guardian in your home, I would also ask you to consider the following: Any breeder of "quality" Bullmastiffs will tell you that the breed is slow to mature. It is two or even three years from the time the animal is born before you can expect the average dog to work well as a guardian. If you are lucky, the dog will probably be dead five or six years later. Compare the number of actual working years that you get out of a Bullmastiff to the twelve or more years that another breed will give you, then ask yourself if you really want a Bullmastiff.

In struggling to find something positive to say about this breed, let me say that I have never known one to hurt a child. My poor Bullmastiff loved my boys. It is an incredibly powerful, fun-loving dog that will serve very well as a companion for as long as its health holds up. It has also got to be one of the best deterrents against crime in the canine world, as the appearance of the breed is downright awesome. If

this sounds like enough to you, go find yourself a Bullmastiff. If you do, I hope you enjoy it— *but* never tell anyone you bought it based upon my recommendation.

Standard for the Bullmastiff

GENERAL APPEARANCE—That of a symmetrical animal showing great strength; powerfully built but active. The dog is fearless yet docile, has endurance and alertness. The foundation breeding was 60% Mastiff and 40% Bulldog.

HEAD—Skull large, with a fair amount of wrinkle when alert; broad, with cheeks well developed. Forehead flat. Muzzle broad and deep; its length, in comparison with that of the entire head, is approximately as 1 is to 3. Lack of foreface with nostrils set on top of muzzle is a reversion to the Bulldog and is very undesirable. Nose black with nostrils large and broad. Flews not too pendulous; stop moderate; and the mouth (bite) preferably level or slightly undershot. Canine teeth large and set wide apart. A dark muzzle is preferable.
Eyes—Dark and of medium size
Ears—V-shaped and carried

close to the cheeks, set on wide and high, level with occiput and cheeks, giving a square appearance to the skull; darker in color than the body and medium in size.

NECK—Slightly arched, of moderate length, very muscular, and almost equal in circumference to the skull.

BODY—Compact. Chest wide and deep, with ribs well sprung and well set down between the forelegs.

FOREQUARTERS—Shoulders muscular but not loaded, and slightly sloping. Forelegs straight, well boned and set well apart; elbows square, pasterns straight, feet of medium size, with rounded toes well arched. Pads thick and tough, nails black.

BACK—Short, giving the impression of a well balanced dog.

LOINS—Wide, muscular and slightly arched, with fair depth of flank.

HINDQUARTERS—Broad and muscular with well developed second thigh denoting power, but not cumbersome. Moderate angulation at hocks. Cowhocks and splay feet are bad faults.

TAIL—Set on high, strong at the root and tapering to the hocks. It may be straight or curved, but never carried hound fashion.

COAT—Short and dense, giving good weather protection.

Color—Red, fawn or brindle. Except for a very small white spot on the chest, white marking is considered a fault.

SIZE—Dogs, 25 to 27 inches at the shoulder, and 110 to 130 pounds weight. Bitches, 24 to 26 inches at the shoulder, and 100 to 120 pounds weight. Other things being equal, the heavier dog is favored.

A very pale color phase for the Bullmastiff but otherwise a healthy-looking young dog.

THE BULL TERRIER

The author must admit to a certain fondness of all the bull-and-terrier breeds, especially the American Pit Bull Terrier, the American Staffordshire Terrier, the Staffordshire Bull Terrier (not discussed in this book due to its very small size), and the Bull Terrier. As a result, I am not sure whether I should or should not offer a word of warning that the Bull Terrier is often too small to be considered a true man-stopper, even though it is a great protection dog. On the one hand, the Bull Terrier is small (50 to 65 pounds or so); on the other hand, it is truly "100 pounds of power in a 50-pound bag." Much like its relative, the Pit Bull, this is a breed with

THE BULL TERRIER

The Bull Terrier can be one heck of a guard dog in spite of its size and fun-loving appearance. Owner, George Schreiber.

great speed, incredible strength and determination which is nothing short of awesome. If a Bull Terrier decides it is very mad at you (and it will definitely decide this if you attack its master or intrude upon its home), you will have to kill the dog to stop it from attacking you. Quitting a battle is an unknown concept to any of the bull-terrier breeds. Considering the speed, agility, overall power and jaw strength of these dogs, one will be hard pressed to destroy a Bull Terrier before one is seriously injured. However, I could not imagine not eventually defeating an attacking Bull Terrier. Since I seem to be at a loss for the ability to criticize these dogs in any way, you decide whether or not this meets your description of a man-stopper.

The history of the Bull Terrier is much the same as the history of the American Pit Bull Terrier and the American Staffordshire Terrier. The original cross between the bulldog of Elizabethan times and the terrier had proven to be a successful one in that, from this cross, the greatest fighting dogs in the world were produced. Recognizing this, in 1850, James Hinks of Birmingham, England, decided that it might be interesting to try crossing the bull-and-terrier dog back to the terrier, for purposes of both improving the fighting ability of the dog and improving its overall appearance. Hinks used the now extinct White English Terrier in his experiment to further enhance the white coat of the breed—some say that he may have also used Dalmatian and Pointer blood. (I must add that, on a personal note, I find this very difficult to believe, as no man who is interested in the

THE BULL TERRIER

pit-fighting ability of his line would ever consider such a contradictory admixture.) Hinks had high hopes for his dogs, both as fighters and as show pieces, and he made claims concerning their abilities, which time and the dog pits have shown to be false. Hinks boasted that to prove the fighting ability of his Bull Terriers, he matched one against a bull-and-terrier dog, and, after it had defeated its opponent, it was so unmarked by this easy victory that it went on to win a conformation show that same day. Historical literature refers to the victory often, but this isolated victory, if it ever occurred, was not a meaningful one.

Although the Bull Terrier, as it was developed by James Hinks, never achieved great success against the half-and-half dogs in the English pits, it did achieve success in the rat pits.

Much of the appeal of this unique breed is captured in this family portrait: ineffable beauty. Photo by Isabelle Français.

THE BULL TERRIER

A good Bull Terrier head. Handler, Stephen Wojculewski.

Achieving success in the rat pits involved killing as many rats as possible in the shortest period of time as spectators looked on. Incredible records were set by Bull Terriers in the rat pits. One dog is said to have killed a hundred rats in just over six minutes, while another is said to have killed five hundred rats in an hour and a half.

In spite of this success, however, the Bull Terrier, or the White Cavalier, as the breed came to be called, probably owes its survival more to its popularity as a gentleman's dog than as a fighter. The British gentry class thought it most fashionable to be seen with a cane in one hand and a Bull Terrier leashed to

the other.

Throughout this period, it was only the pure-white Bull Terrier, as developed by James Hinks, that interested breeders and show dog enthusiasts. In 1921, Dr. William A. Bruethe says of the Bull Terrier, in his *Complete Dog Book*, that there existed a movement among Bull Terrier enthusiasts to bring back Bull Terriers that were brindle and other colors. By 1936, the Colored Bull Terrier was voted a separate variety of the breed by the A.K.C. These dogs were not created by simply selecting for a colored coat among white litters but rather by breeding the show version of the white Staffordshire Bull Terrier (or the half-and-half dog) back to the terrier. In essence these coat types are shown separately today, as they are indeed somewhat different breeds. At the present time, however, there are some show enthusiasts who do not agree with showing these Bull Terriers separately, and one might begin to expect that it will not be long before they are shown as one breed in response to this sentiment.

Whether you choose a Colored or a White Bull Terrier as a guard dog, it is certain that you will select more dog than most intruders bargain for. The dogs are extremely capable for their size, but, in spite of their capability, they really don't offer the deterrent effect that a larger breed might. If space is no problem and a guard dog is called for, one of the larger

Jumping for fun and a stick. Owner, George Schreiber.

man-stopping breeds might be better suited for the job, but, if a small home or apartment is all the room you have, you would do well to give some thought to owning a good, strong Bull Terrier.

Standard for the Bull Terrier

WHITE:

GENERAL APPEARANCE—The Bull Terrier must be strongly built, muscular, symmetrical and active, with a keen, determined and intelligent expression, full of fire but of sweet disposition and amenable to discipline.

HEAD—The head should be long, strong and deep right to the end of the muzzle, but not coarse. Full face, it should be oval in outline and be filled completely up giving the impression of fullness with a surface devoid of hollows or indentations, *i.e.*, egg-shaped. In profile it should curve gently downwards from the top of the skull to the tip of the nose. The forehead should be flat across from ear to ear. The distance from the tip of the nose to the eyes should be perceptibly greater than that from the eyes to the top of the skull. The underjaw should be deep and well defined.

Lips—The lips should be clean and tight.

Teeth—The teeth should meet in either a level or a scissors bite. In the scissors bite, the upper teeth should fit in front of and closely against the lower teeth, and they should be sound, strong

White Bull Terriers have a distintive appearance and appeal. Owners, Irene and Tom Lecki.

I took this picture of this Bull Terrier. This is among my very favorite breeds of all.

and perfectly regular.

Ears—The ears should be small, thin and placed close together. They should be capable of being held stiffly erect when they point upwards.

Eyes—The eyes should be well sunken and as dark as possible, with a piercing glint. They should be small, triangular, and obliquely placed; set near together and high up on the head. Blue eyes are a disqualification.

Nose—The nose should be black, with well-developed

135

nostrils bent downward at the tip.

NECK—The neck should be very muscular, long, arched and clean, tapering from the shoulders to the head and it should be free from loose skin.

BODY—The body should be well rounded with marked spring of rib, the back should be short and strong. The back ribs deep. Slightly arched over the loin. The shoulders should be strong and muscular but without heaviness. The shoulder blades should be wide and flat and there should be a very pronounced backward slope from the bottom edge of the blade to the top edge. Behind the shoulders there should be no slackness or dip at the withers. The underline from the brisket to the belly should form a graceful upward curve.

Chest—The chest should be broad when viewed from in front, and there should be great depth from withers to brisket, so that the latter is nearer the ground than the belly.

Legs—The legs should be big boned but not to the point of coarseness; the forelegs should be of moderate length, perfectly straight, and the dog must stand firmly upon them. The elbows must turn neither in nor out, and the pasterns should be strong and upright. The hind legs should be parallel when viewed from behind. The thighs very muscular with hocks well let down. Hind pasterns short and upright. The stifle joint should be well bent with a well-developed second thigh.

Feet—The feet should be round and compact with well-arched toes like a cat.

TAIL—The tail should be short, set on low, fine, and ideally should be carried horizontally. It should be thick where it joins the body, and should taper to a fine point.

COAT—The coat should be short, flat, harsh to the touch and have a fine gloss. The skin should fit tightly.

Color—The color is white though markings on the head are permissible. Any markings elsewhere on the coat are to be severely faulted. Skin pigmentations are not to be penalized.

GAIT—The dog shall move smoothly, covering the ground with free, easy strides, fore and hind legs should move parallel each to each when viewed from front or back. The forelegs reaching out well and the hind legs moving smoothly at the hip and flexing well at the stifle and hock. The dog should move compactly and in one piece but with a typical jaunty air that suggests agility and power.

FAULTS—Any departure from the foregoing points shall be considered a fault and the seriousness of the fault shall be in exact proportion to its degree, *i.e.*, a very crooked front is a very bad fault; a rather crooked front is a rather bad fault; and a slightly crooked front is a slight fault.

COLORED: The standard for the Colored variety is the same as for the White except for the category "Color" which reads:

COLOR—Any color other than white, or any color with white markings. Other things being equal, the preferred color is brindle. A dog which is predominantly white shall be disqualified.

The Bull Terrier's head must be strong and deep to the end of the muzzle. Photo by Robert Pearcy.

THE CANARY DOG

Above: At home this behemoth is known as el Perro de Presa Canario.

Suppose I were to ask you what the Canary Islands of Spain were originally named after. You probably would guess that the islands were named after the canary birds that were found living wild on the islands. This would be a good but inaccurate guess. In fact, the Canary Islands were named after the large dogs that were originally found on the islands (can = dogs), and the birds took their name from the

Opposite: If the Canary Dog doesn't become relatively popular in the U.S., we are making a big mistake.

islands.

On the Canary Islands, this dog is known as the Perro de Presa Canario (Dog of Prey of the Canary Islands), but I have decided that coining the breed name "Canary Dog" would be more useful for our purposes. As such, if you are reading this for the first time and are worried that you have never before heard of this breed, stop worrying, add the Canary Dog to your mental list of useful purebreds. It certainly deserves such a position.

Specifically, the Canary Dog is indigenous to the islands of Tenerife and Gran Canario of Spain's Canary Islands. It is primarily a country dog, although due to a recent increase in the popularity of the breed it can now be found throughout the islands. An old friend of mine recently booked a vacation to Tenerife and, before he left, I asked him to keep an eye out for Canary Dogs in populated areas. I showed him exactly what to look for and asked him to snap a few pictures of whatever dogs he found. Upon his return, I learned that he had come across two native Canary Dogs as he was walking down the street in a very "touristy" area. Each of these two was with a different owner.

The Canary Dog was originally produced by the crossing of mastiffs and bulldogs, brought to the islands by English settlers during the nineteenth century, to the native Canary Island dogs.

Among the native dogs, the most important was the Bardino Majero, a dog which originated on the Isla Fuerteventura.

The Bardino Majero was a farm dog, probably of pre-Hispanic development, found amply scattered throughout the archipelago. It was valuable as a country working dog and known to be easy going and even-tempered around its owners but quite fierce around strangers. Its coat was of medium length and it was not a robust breed, but anything it lacked in body it made up for in courage and dedication.

The crossbreeding of the Bardino Majero to the mastiffs and bulldogs of England produced a very large, powerfully built dog that was normally either brindle or fawn in color and usually displayed white patches on the chest and feet. These original crossbred dogs were known far and wide for their great courage, strength, and ferocity.

At the time that the mastiffs and bulldogs of England were being crossed with the Bardino Majero on the islands of Tenerife and Gran Canario, organized dogfighting was very popular throughout the archipelago. As one would expect, the inhabitants of the Canary Islands were hardly unique in their enthusiasm for this bloody sport. Much of Western Europe was involved in this activity, either in plain view of the law or underground; in France, for

THE CANARY DOG

"I would like to see these dogs become popular throughout the world, and I would also like to see fanciers of this breed draw from good stock for ownership"

example, the dogfights drew large crowds of spectators. It was for its participation in these matches that the Canary Dog was most highly regarded. The selective breeding of these dogs was conducted with nothing but potential accomplishment in the arena in mind.

By the time organized dogfighting became prohibited throughout the archipelago in 1940, the Perro de Presa Canario had long since been perfected both as a purebred and as a fighting dog of great acclaim. At a body size of just over 100 pounds, these incredibly game, powerful, and determined animals were a match for any dog in the world. So highly prized by the dogfighting fraternity of the islands were these dogs and the sport that in spite of the prohibition of dogfighting, the activity continued underground. Purebred stock did become more and more rare, however, as the breeding of the many dogs not used for fighting became lax.

During the 1960s, the German Shepherd Dog was introduced to the Canary Islands for the first time. Its popularity as a companion and a guard dog grew in leaps and bounds, due to the breed's great reputation. At this time, the popularity of the Canary Dog was at an all-time low. Thus, the German Shepherd's introduction dealt the native breed another damaging blow, and, by the end of the 1960s, the Canary Dog was right on

the edge of extinction in its pure form.

Fortunately, at the beginning of the 1970s, there was a great resurgence of interest in the Canary Dog on the part of the Spanish rare breed enthusiasts who lived through the breed's transitional stages and who knew these dogs to be well worthy of preservation. The breeding of pure-blooded Canary Dogs became more common, and it wasn't long before these veteran breeders introduced younger breeders to the fancy.

By 1975, the population of good Canary Dog stock began to grow rapidly, and by 1982, the breed was being shown by serious show enthusiasts on the islands. Fanciers of this breed are quite clear in their opinion that, although the Perro de Presa Canario is very useful as a cattle dog and especially as a guard dog, today's show breeders must never forget that this breed was originally a fighting dog—and it is the general qualities of a fighting dog that the breed must always display.

I have been fortunate in that I have communicated quite extensively with the president of the club that is promoting these dogs in Spain. This communication has allowed me to gain a great deal of insight into the breed, and it is one of my goals to pass this insight on to purebred fanciers around the world. At one point, I was offered a young pair of the finest Canary Dogs available;

and while I was very tempted to accept the offer, I was not in the market for two dogs at the time, but rather only one. I did not want to take one (even if the promoters of the breed would have let me have only one), as it is much more important that these dogs be exported in pairs only and that they be made accessible to serious breeders only. I would like to see these dogs become popular throughout the world, and I would also like to see fanciers of this breed draw from good stock for ownership. *Now* is the time for serious breeders of rare purebreds to take an interest in the Canary Dog.

As a guardian breed with man-stopping ability, there is no dog that is more effective than the Canary Dog. It remains an incredibly powerful and fearless animal, it is known for its great devotion to its human family, and it is known to accept children in the home. This is a dog that will stay by its master's side at all times and is never known to stray. This dog is protective by nature and will not hesitate to attack

The Canary Dog—a breed I can tell you I named myself and introduced to the States.

The Perro de Presa Canario, or Canary Dog, "serves very well as a guard dog and is generally quite ferocious toward strangers."

anyone whom it perceives as a threat to its family or home. Such an attack could only be a hopeless situation for any man involved.

A strange story that I have heard more than once in reference to these dogs—one that is so strange it warrants repeating here—involves untrained Canary Dogs attacking the wheels of passing automobiles. While this is a habit that any breed will develop if left unchained and not discouraged from the activity (we have all seen it many times), such an attack from a Canary Dog takes a new twist. Apparently, these dogs are so fast and their jaws are so powerful that they will actually grab and hold the spinning wheel of a passing car and, as the wheel continues to turn, the dog's head is spun around and is quickly squashed beneath the car! A number of these dogs have lost their lives in this manner, and, while the story does not have a happy ending, it certainly speaks highly for the physical ability of the Canary Dog. I guess the moral is, if I am successful in interesting a number of people in these dogs and if we do eventually establish our own population, we had better teach them quickly not to chase cars.

In all seriousness, I do urge the rare breed enthusiasts among my readers to investigate this breed carefully. Establish contacts in Spain (e.g., the Spanish Kennel Club via the American Kennel Club).

Ask for the "Club Español de Los Molosos de Arena" in Madrid, and import these fine dogs in breeding pairs. These are exceptional guard dogs as well as being exceptional companion dogs, and they certainly have their place among established purebreds. I am sure that enthusiasts will quickly recognize the value of the breed upon its introduction.

Standard for the Perro de Presa Canario

GENERAL DESCRIPTION—The Canary Dog is a gentle and affectionate dog that displays great respect for its human family. It serves very well as a guard dog and is generally quite ferocious toward strangers. It is normally very aggressive toward other dogs, and this aggressiveness displays its fighting ancestry. Its bark is deep and low.

HEAD—The Canary Dog has a powerful looking head that is practically as wide as it is long. The proportion of the head to the face is generally six to four, although the face can be slightly shorter. The stop is pronounced.

Mask and Nose—Both the nose and the mask are black.

Eyes and Eyelids—The eyelids should be black. The eyes are slightly oval in shape and should be well separated from each

THE CANARY DOG

other. The eye color ranges from medium to dark chestnut, depending upon the color of the coat. The shade must not be darker than hazel, however. Lighter shades are not desirable.

Ears—These dogs have high set ears that are of medium size and hang. Cropped ears are acceptable in keeping with the accuracy of the history of the dog as fighters.

Teeth—The base line of the implant is very strong and generally well set in. Given the breed's origin, a slightly undershot bite is acceptable. The upper lips hang and cover the lower lips.

NECK—The neck is broad, powerful, and truncated. Some loose skin on the underside is typical. The neck arches slightly from the head to the back.

BODY

Rump—The rump forms a clear angle in relation to the dorsal lumbar line and falls gently forming a curve. The height of the rump is generally a centimeter higher than the height of the dog at the withers.

Chest—Between the front legs, the chest is wide, low, and deep. The ribs build the chest as a broad cylindrical structure that displays an ability to breathe deeply.

Belly—Well tucked up.

TAIL—The tail is set high. It is thick at the root and tapers to a point at the tip. Its length is such that it reaches the dog's hocks. At rest, the tail hangs slightly to the side, and when the dog is in motion the tail is raised like a cutlass.

LEGS—Well set, well muscled, and strong. Should display heavy bone.

FEET—Cat footed. The nails vary in color depending upon the color of the dog. Darker dogs display darker nails.

COAT—The coat is short and fairly rough. It is generally thicker and stiffer toward the rump. These dogs are either fawn in color or of various shades of brindle. The hide is thick, elastic and loose.

HEIGHT—At the withers, males are 59–65 cm (23¼–25½ inches), females range 55–61 cm (21½–24 inches). Generally, these dogs are 5 cm longer than they are tall at the withers.

WEIGHT—Males: 92–106 pounds. Females: 84–99 pounds.

"Now is the time for serious breeders of rare purebreds to take an interest in the Canary Dog."

THE DOBERMAN PINSCHER

The history of the Doberman Pinscher is both very interesting and amusing to those of us inclined to find humor in historical reconstruction. The breed is named after Herr Louis Dobermann of Apolda, who lived in Thueringen, Germany. During the 1880s, Herr Dobermann held the position of tax collector for his area.

THE DOBERMAN PINSCHER

In those days, being a tax collector involved actually going from door to door collecting taxes. It tells us quite a bit about the willingness of people to pay taxes when we learn that Dobermann felt not only that he needed the accompaniment of a ferocious guard dog in the performance of his duty as tax collector but also that this dog should be such an exceptional guard that none of the breeds then available in Germany were good enough for him. (Keep in mind that some fine guardian breeds were available.) Therefore, Louis Dobermann set out to create his own guardian breed that he felt would perform to his satisfaction.

Fortunately for Dobermann, he had two jobs. His second job was that of dog catcher. As dog catcher, he could bring home any dog he felt would be useful to his breeding program. Some of the breeds used by Dobermann were the Rottweiler, the old German Pinscher, and the Manchester Terrier. It is probable that other "component" breeds were also

used, but it is unclear as to precisely which breeds they were.

Dobermann fixed his breed type quickly and the breed he created worked as well as he had hoped (at least I am unaware of any poundings that Dobermann received at the hands of irate taxpayers once his breed had been perfected). By 1899, Germany's National Doberman Pinscher Club was organized by Otto Goeller, and by 1900 the breed was officially recognized and its written standard was accepted.

Around the year 1908,

Doberman Pinscher dogs began being imported into the United States, and in February of 1921, the Doberman Pinscher Club of America was founded. Today some of the finest show-quality Dobermans are produced by American breeders, while some of the greatest working Dobermans are still being produced in Germany.

The story of the modern-day Doberman Pinscher is at once a great success story and also the story of poor breeding practices. The breed has achieved such great heights of

These are smart and industrious animals, in addition to being strong and beautiful. Owners, Linda and John Krukar.

popularity that breeders involved in the production of these dogs range from the world's most serious, knowledgeable, and sincere, to the most insincere and profit-motivated people imaginable. This breed has achieved the highest honors ever bestowed upon show or protection dogs. One may also count among the ranks of Doberman Pinschers some of the most scatterbred curs ever to be referred to as purebred. What has caused this great range of quality among Dobermans?

We might begin to answer this question by pointing to two factors which have played major roles in the decreased level of general quality among these dogs. These factors are tremendous popularity and misrepresentation of the breed, leading to the breed's bad reputation.

Today the Doberman Pinscher is one of the more popular purebreds in the world. The reasons for this popularity are many, and they include the easy-to-care for short coat of the breed, the relatively convenient size of the dogs (as compared to some of the other

guardian breeds), the reputation for intelligence, and especially, the reputation of this breed as one of the world's finest man-stopping guard dogs. While this may all sound very positive, the fact of the matter is that this popularity has brought the Doberman Pinscher into the hands of very many unknowledgeable and inexperienced dog owners and breeders. In addition, the popularity of the breed has created a tremendous demand for Doberman puppies, which has unfortunately inspired many of these completely irresponsible breeders to turn any two Dobermans of opposite sex into puppy factories. The percentage of very poorly bred Doberman Pinschers among the population of these dogs has increased steadily for many years now. You must choose a breeder very carefully before selecting a Doberman puppy, as you are more likely to find yourself stuck with a poorly

Give me the right Dobie pup and I'd love to own him. I wouldn't mind owning a Macaw or two either. Owner, Marcos Hotz of Brazil.

bred Doberman than almost any other breed available today. Pick and choose carefully, and you can also select the finest of show and protection dogs from among the ranks of Doberman Pinschers.

One can easily be tempted to place the blame on Hollywood for the poor reputation of the Doberman breed as a bloodthirsty scatterbrain with a marked tendency to "turn on its master." While many low-level movies have contributed to this negatively biased perception of the breed, people who consistently try to force the Doberman, against its nature, into becoming an irrational biting machine are primarily responsible. Unfortunately, crazy people who are in search of a crazy dog to complement their personalities have a tendency to select the Doberman as the breed for them. The dog is then raised in an irresponsible manner, learning that the easiest way to please its master is to snarl at anyone it sees. Hence, the reputation of the Doberman as a vicious breed generally reinforces itself among the casual observers of dogs. Again, this reputation appeals only to the people who should never own dogs in the first place, and these people end up not only owning but often breeding Dobermans, and thus the quality of the breed is delivered yet another blow. Steer as far clear as possible from breeders like these and support instead dealers who are working to build a serious reputation in the show and working dog world.

Remember, your Doberman puppy, ounce obtained, will undoubtedly be living with you for many years to come. A little discretion in the beginning will be greatly rewarded later on.

A good Doberman, once selected, is often a very good guard dog. The breed is generally intelligent and discriminating, accepting

The Doberman's reputation as a "vicious" breed has been nurtured by crazy people promoting and breeding a dog as unbalanced as themselves; avoid these harmful, brainless types and seek out fanciers dedicated to the Doberman as a working and show dog.

The best Dobies are among the best of all guard dogs. Attack training requires professional supervision if it is to be executed with success. *Top:* Nanci Little. *Bottom:* Owners, John and Rita Armonia.

An uncropped Doberman has a distinctly different appearance than a cropped one. While I don't care for the practice of ear cropping, in the U.S. it is largely an owner's decision. In Great Britain and other European nations, the practice is prohibited. Owner, D. Eschbach.

friends as friends and intruders as such. The breed is not only quick thinking and very alert, but fast moving and very well balanced. It is a strong dog and, as such, a sizeable Doberman does qualify as an effective man-stopping guardian. The strength of this breed has been grossly overrated by the general public, however, and the breed should never be expected to display the kind of power displayed by many of the other breeds in this book. If you are anticipating an all-out, winner-take-all, fight-to-the-finish, frontal attack by a large man, you might consider opting for one of the more powerful breeds. In addition, the Doberman will not commonly display a willingness to continue an attack once it becomes clear that it is overpowered or once it gets seriously hurt in combat, as will some of the other breeds discussed here. Finally, the Doberman Pinscher has become so common lately and the breed is represented by so many poorly bred, functionless individuals that simply having a Doberman on one's premises is not nearly the deterrent to crime that it once was.

Once again, a well-chosen Doberman is an excellent pet and an excellent guard. For almost all practical purposes, it offers the ability and the deterrent effect necessary to keep a home safe. It is a beautiful breed and, if you are inclined to appreciate its form of beauty, a well-chosen Doberman is a wise choice as a home guardian. Finally, I cannot stress enough the importance of selecting your dealer carefully. Unless you are very knowledgeable in this area, I firmly advise discussing the question of reputable dealers thoroughly with your

A typical Dobie smile on a typical Dobie. Owners, Annie and Daniel Mulero of Brazil.

The Doberman is a very trainable dog as well as being a natural guardian—when he's good, that is. Photo by Mae Downing. Owner, Gertrude Payant of Canada.

national registry or breed club. A call is cheap, but living with a poorly bred dog can be very disappointing.

Standard for the Doberman Pinscher

GENERAL APPEARANCE—The appearance is that of a dog of medium size, with a body that is square; the height, measured vertically from the ground to the highest point of the withers, equalling the length measured horizontally from the forechest to the rear projection of the upper thigh. Length of head, neck and legs in proportion to length and depth of body. Compactly built, muscular and powerful, for great endurance and speed. Elegant in appearance, of proud carriage, reflecting great nobility and temperament. Energetic, watchful, determined, alert, fearless, loyal and obedient. **Faults**—The judge shall dismiss from the ring any shy or vicious Doberman. **Shyness**—A dog shall be judged fundamentally shy if, refusing to stand for examination, it shrinks away from the judge; if it fears an approach from the rear; if it shies at sudden and unusual noises to a marked degree. **Viciousness**—A dog that attacks or attempts to attack either the judge or its handler is definitely vicious. An aggressive or belligerent attitude towards other dogs shall not be deemed viciousness.

HEIGHT—At the withers a dog is 26 to 28 inches, ideally about 27½ inches. A bitch is 24 to 26 inches with 25½ inches the ideal.

HEAD—Long and dry, resembling a blunt wedge in both frontal and profile views. When seen from the front, the head widens gradually toward the base of the ears in a practically unbroken line. Top of skull flat, turning with a slight stop to bridge of muzzle, with muzzle line extending parallel to top line of skull. Cheeks flat and muscular. Lips lying close to jaws. Jaws full and powerful, well filled under the eyes. *Eyes*—Almond shaped, moderately deep set, with vigorous, energetic

Right: My friend Eddie Dombish (or his lower half, anyway) working a Dobie. Eddie is a great trainer based in New York City. *Opposite:* In profile and from the front, the Doberman's muzzle should appear as a blunt wedge. Photo by Robert Pearcy.

This Dobie has the look of a bird of prey. It tells you all that you need to know about the breed at a glance. Photo by Alton Anderson. This is Ch. Damasyn Bo-Tairic of Ardon, owned by Peggy Adamson.

expression. Iris of uniform color, ranging from medium to darkest brown in black dogs; in reds, blues, and fawns the color of the iris blends with that of the markings, the darkest shade being preferable in every case. *Teeth*—Strongly developed and white. Lower incisors upright and touching inside of upper incisors. A true scissors bite. 42 correctly placed teeth, 22 in the lower, 20 in the upper jaw. Distemper teeth shall not be penalized. **Faults**— Overshot more than ³⁄₁₆ of an inch. Undershot more than ⅛ of an inch. Four or more missing teeth. All the aforementioned are considered disqualifying. *Ears*—Normally cropped and carried erect. The upper attachment of the

Firmness and musculature are paramount in the conformation ring. This is Ch. Wynterwynd's Me N' My Shadow, owned by Phil and Jill Leath.

ear, when held erect, is on a level with the top of the skull.

Nose—Solid black on black dogs, dark brown on red ones, dark gray on blue ones, dark tan on fawns.

NECK—Proudly carried, well muscled and dry. Well arched with nape of neck widening gradually towards body.

BODY—Back short, firm, of sufficient width, and muscular at the loins, extending in a straight line from withers to the *slightly* rounded croup.

Withers—Pronounced and forming the highest point of the body.

Brisket—Reaching deep to the elbow.

Chest—Broad with forechest well defined.

Ribs—Well sprung from the spine, but flattened in lower end to permit elbow clearance.

Belly—Well tucked up, extending in a curved line from the brisket.

Loins—Wide and muscled.

Hips—Broad and in proportion to body, breadth of hips approximately equal to breadth of body at rib cage and shoulders.

TAIL—Docked at approximately second joint, appears to be a continuation of the spine, and is carried only slightly above the horizontal when the dog is alert.

The conformation and physique of a working dog like the Doberman cannot be underestimated.

FOREQUARTERS

Shoulder Blade—Sloping forward and downward at a 45-degree angle to the ground meets the upper arm at an angle of 90 degrees. Length of shoulder blade and upper arm are equal. Height from elbow to the withers approximately equals height from ground to elbow.

Legs—Seen from front and side, perfectly straight and parallel to each other from elbow to pastern; muscled and sinewy with heavy bone. In normal pose and when gaiting, the elbows lie close to the brisket.

Pasterns—Firm and almost perpendicular to the ground.

Feet—Well arched, compact, and catlike, turning neither in nor out. Dewclaws may be removed.

HINDQUARTERS—The angulation of the hindquarters balances that of the forequarters.

Hip Bone—Falls away from spinal column at an angle of about 30 degrees, producing a slightly rounded, well filled-out croup.

Upper Shanks—At right angles to the hip bones, are long, wide, and well muscled on both sides of thigh with clearly defined stifles. Upper and lower shanks are of equal length.

While the dog is at rest, hock to heel is perpendicular to the ground. Viewed from the rear, the legs are straight, parallel to each other, and wide enough apart to fit in with a properly built body.

Feet—Cat feet as on front legs, turning neither in nor out. Dewclaws, if any, are generally removed.

GAIT—Free, balanced and vigorous, with good reach in the forequarters and good driving power in the hindquarters. When trotting, there is a strong rear-action drive. Each rear leg moves in line with the foreleg on the same side. Rear and front legs are thrown neither in nor out. Back remains strong and firm. When moving at a fast trot, a properly built dog will single-track.

COAT—Smooth-haired, short, hard, thick and close lying. Invisible gray undercoat on neck permissible.

Color—Allowed are black, red, blue, and fawn (Isabella).

Markings—Rust, sharply defined, appearing above each eye and on muzzle, throat and forechest, on all legs and feet, and below tail. White patch on chest, not exceeding ½ square inch, permissible. **Fault**—Dogs not of an allowed color.

The shape and fullness of the breed's head are essential to the proper character. Photo by Isabelle Français. Owners, Andrew and Nancy Erny.

THE DOGO ARGENTINO

Opposite: **One of the best, if not** *the* **best, of all guard dogs is the Dogo Argentino.** *Left:* **A solid Dogo placing at the World Dog Show in the mid-1980s. Photo by Isabelle Français. Owner, Gabriel Moyette.**

To date, Argentina has produced only one widely recognized purebred. Originally created as a hunting dog of outstanding capability, the Dogo Argentino was also fashioned to be equally useful as a great guard dog. Known today as the father of the Dogo breed, the late Dr. Antonio Nores Martinez, a dog enthusiast and avid hunter from Argentina, sought to construct a hunting dog of unsurpassable capability to be used solely on the most dangerous game in all of the Americas. It was the wild boar and the big cats, the puma and the jaguar, that the Dogo was to pursue. In the opinion of

If this doesn't look to you like a dog that means business, then you need to re-think your understanding of dogs. Owner, Gabriel Moyette.

Dr. Martinez, no other breed known to man at the time displayed all of the qualities necessary to be effective in the hunting of this ferocious game, particularly in a mountainous environment.

The basic stock with which Dr. Martinez began his breeding program was a group of crossbred dogs that were closely related to each other in terms of ancestry and that were being constructed and used throughout Argentina at the time for purposes of competing in organized dogfights. These crossbred dogs, known

collectively as the "Fighting Dogs of Cordoba" or the "Cordoba Dogs," were sometimes produced by crossing the Spanish Mastiff with the Bull Terrier and sometimes by crossing the Spanish Mastiff to a cross between the Bull Terrier and the old fighting English Bulldog. Some breeders introduced the blood of the German Bulldog or Boxer into their lines as well. As a result of these different methods of producing the old Cordoba Dog, this crossbred dog looked different from others of its type, but all types shared great functional ability as a common characteristic. While the many distinct lines of Cordoba Dog never reached a point in their development at which breeders could refer to these fighting dogs as purebred, the breeding of Cordoba Dogs was very selective, generation after generation, and selection of breeding stock was entirely dependent upon functional capability. The most essential characteristics of the Cordoba Dog were strength, fighting ability, and the willingness to fight to the death, if need be, for the pure sport of the fight.

Dr. Martinez, in turn, was highly selective in his choices of purebreds to breed into the Cordoba Dog. In order to give his dogs added height, he began by breeding in the Great Dane. As the Cordoba Dog was almost always pure white in color, and as this was a characteristic that Dr. Martinez wanted to preserve in his Dogo, he used exclusively Harlequin Great Danes in his breeding program. He also added Pyrenean Mastiff stock in order to give his dogs more size and also accentuate the white coat color of his dogs. He felt that the generally good nose of the Pyrenean Mastiff and its abilty to work well under all climatic conditions would also be useful attributes for his Dogos.

To further increase the dog's tracking ability, the blood of English Pointer was added. Dr. Martinez felt that, with a highly developed sense of smell, the Dogo could track and hunt without having to keep its nose to the ground. Irish Wolfhound blood was also introduced to the Dogo so that

This Dogo belonged to Enrique Sanchirico and I knew it well. It would play with you one minute and tear your head off the next, depending on what Enrique wanted.

the speed of the dog during the hunt would be increased. While Dr. Martinez saw a need to produce a dog that could move quickly on the hunt, he was not overly concerned with producing a dog with the ability of a great coursing hound, as the game that the Dogo was being developed to pursue was not as fast in the long distance as was the game of the coursing hounds.

Finally, Mastiff blood, especially French Mastiff blood (Dogue de Bordeaux), was added to increase the size of the head of the Dogo and to accentuate the dog's courage, overall body strength and jaw strength. The Dogue de Bordeaux, which itself was held

It is said that a Dogo can look like a large white Pit Bull Terrier, proving that "a rose by any other name..." Photo by Isabelle Français.

in high regard in France as a terrific fighting dog, was also being used for similar purposes in Argentina—but there is some question as to whether the Dogue in Argentina was a purebred.

In any event, Dr. Martinez produced a very powerful and capable dog, but his breeding program was far from being finished. In order to avoid what he felt would be the harmful effects of consanguinity, Martinez established two entirely separate lines of Dogos, one which he called the Araucanian line and the other which he called the Guarani family. Many of his

"component" breeds were also reintroduced later on for further breeding in order to freshen up his lines.

As the breed began to grow in numbers, the problem of consanguinity diminished in Martinez's view. By 1928, Dr. Martinez had developed a written breed standard, by which he judged his dogs, but functional ability remained the overriding factor according to which breeding stock was selected.

As a hunter of the boar, the jaguar, and the puma, the Dogo proved to be a great dog. As difficult as this may be for some of us to believe, today's Dogo is

Believe me, if it's a guard dog you're after, the Dogo is it. Owner, Gabriel Moyette.

capable of tracking, attacking, and actually killing a puma or jaguar single-handedly. A pack of five Dogos should be capable of bringing down a 450-pound wild boar, although many a Dogo has lost its life in the performance of this feat.

As important as hunting ability was to Dr. Martinez, he also saw a great need to develop the Dogo as the ultimate guard dog. Dr. Martinez felt that, while many so-called guard dogs would bark at, attack, and even bite an intruder, few had the heart to fight an intruder to the death, if need be. In his words, "A dog who attacks an intruder and then, at the first threat of injury, abandons its prisoner is worth nothing as a guardian."

Today the Dogo is used throughout Argentina as both a hunting dog and a guard dog. Many Dogos have found their way to Europe, especially

Germany, and quite a few have gone to the United States via Argentine immigrants. In Europe and the United States, the breed is exclusively a guardian and has proven to be very effective at this job.

I personally have known and actually worked with many Dogos and have found them to be very willing and capable guard dogs. They adapt to guard work as if it were their nature, which it is, and require very little training in this area in order to be useful. At a body weight of 80-105 pounds, and with their short coats and compact bodies, they are suitable for home or apartment use, and they are also very suitable as family dogs. If I am asked to point to any problem areas in this breed, I might add that while Dr. Martinez intended the breed to be basically quiet, and while most Dogos are quiet dogs, when one

Here I am judging Dogos at a rare breed show in New Jersey. To the best of my knowledge, they had never been judged in the U.S. before.

decides to bark it can shake a ceiling down. In addition, I would be careful where I bought a Dogo, as some dealers are not as careful to avoid congenital problems as are others.

from the parent breeds are a masterful blend resulting in a large, powerful dog with great endurance. The Dogo should give the appearance of an elegant, smoothly muscled, well-balanced dog

Standard for the Dogo Argentino

GENERAL DESCRIPTION—The Dogo Argentino is bred in his native Argentina to hunt big game, primarily boar and mountain lion. He hunts great distances over rugged terrain and engages the game until the hunter kills it. He is one breed developed from ten. The many attributes

capable of stepping out of the ring and into the hunt. Judges are asked by the club sponsoring the breed to keep this fact uppermost in their minds when evaluating the merits of the dog.

HEAD—Massive skull. When viewed from the front the skull is square in shape with chiseled features, a furrow between the eyes and pronounced cheek muscles. When viewed in profile, the distance from the tip of the

These are agile, well-built dogs, with a lot of capability. Photo by Isabelle Français.

nose to the stop is equal to the distance from the stop to occiput.

Muzzle—The nasal bone is so formed that the nose is slightly higher at the tip than the muzzle at the stop.

Eyes—Eyes are preferably dark or hazel in color. Eyelids rimmed in any color from black to pink.

Another of Enrique's dogs, this Dogo is named "Puma."

Black being preferred. The expression is alive and intelligent but with a remarkable intensity at the same time.

Nose—Nostrils well developed and wide open. Black in color. Pink on the nose is permissible provided the majority of the nose is black.

Lips—Close fitting, edged

with black. Note: Close fitting lips are required to permit the Dogo to breathe through the corners of the mouth when holding prey.

Jaws—Well fitted, neither undershot nor overshot. Strong with large teeth similarly shaped and sized. The four canine teeth must be especially large and clean, meshing perfectly when the jaws are closed. The number of molars is not important.

Ears—Cropped, set high on head, triangular in shape.

NECK—Thick, arched and flexible with the skin at the throat very thick. The crest of the neck should flow to the base of the skull without the occipital bone being prominent. Note: The skin must be loose to permit it to slide over the body so that in fighting the teeth or claws of the prey wound only the skin and not the flesh. Flexibility of the skin over the throat permits the Dogo to move rapidly to grab prey.

CHEST—Quite broad, deep and well muscled extending below the elbows.

SHOULDERS—Muscular and well laid back.

FORELEGS—Straight with upright pasterns.

FEET—Length of toes in proportion with feet, well arched and closely spaced. Pads are thick and tough.

BACK—The back is strong with well-developed muscles. The loin of the back is the highest curving gently towards the croup.

HINDQUARTERS—
Muscular and powerful with good angulation. Hocks well let down. Dewclaws, if any, are to be removed. Note: The hindquarters must be very muscular since the speed of the Dogo and his ability to hold his prey are dependent upon this.

TAIL—Long and thick. The tail does not extend beyond the hock. At rest the tail is carried down and when in chase or combat with prey the tail is carried up.

COAT—Very short and thick, smooth and glossy.

Color—White. Markings on the head are permissible. Any markings elsewhere on the coat are to be severely faulted. Skin pigmentation is not to be penalized.

WEIGHT—82 to 95 pounds.

HEIGHT—23½ to 25½ inches at the shoulder. All other points being equal the taller, heavier Dogo is to be preferred provided he is balanced.

DISQUALIFICATIONS—
Blue or China eyes. Deafness. Noticeably undershot or overshot bite.

Loose lips hanging below lower jaw. Uncropped ears. Long hair. Height under 23½ inches.

Dogo Argentino Club of America, 1985

Enrique Sanchirico, a great guy with a great dog.

173

THE DOGUE DE BORDEAUX

Opposite: Scary and reptilian—whatever images this awesome dog conjures should remain with a person for years to come. This is "Ursule" at 11 months.

The Dogue de Bordeaux, often referred to as the Bordeaux Dogue, the Bordeaux Mastiff, the Dogue, or sometimes even the French Bulldog (the latter breed name causing confusion at times), is beyond a shadow of a doubt one of the greatest man-stopping guard dogs in the world. The breed has existed in the south of France for centuries, perhaps millenia, and inasmuch as the appearance of these dogs is quite distinct, we can easily say that the Dogue de Bordeaux is indigenous to

Above: Solid through and through, the Dogue de Bordeaux is a fearsome guardian dog of France. This is "Uhl."

France.

The author has taken a particular interest in this breed not only because the Dogue is so very interesting in its own right but also because it is so ironic that the breed does not yet exist in any significant numbers outside of France and Germany. The irony of the Dogue's unfamiliarity to many purebred enthusiasts lies in the fact that the breed is exactly what so many of us are looking for in a dog.

In general, the Bordeaux Dogue is a very impressive looking animal that radiates raw power as clearly as does any breed in existence today. Its appearance is overshadowed only by its actual ability, which again figures second only to its devotion to its human family, adults and children alike.

The overall appearance of the Bordeaux Dogue is best compared to the Bullmastiff. The body of the Bordeaux Dogue might be a little longer than that of the average Bullmastiff, the head should definitely be larger, the bite should be more undershot, and the coloring different; but, in general, those among us who like the appearance of the Bullmastiff will like the appearance of the Bordeaux Dogue very much.

Temperamentally, the Bordeaux Dogue and the Bullmastiff differ. Most Bordeaux Dogues are born with the temperament that all Bullmastiffs should be born with but too often are not. The Dogue is a no-nonsense breed that, though friendly towards its friends, is dangerous to its enemies. Given its brute strength, there are few dogs that can match this breed's overall suitability as a guard.

Historically, the Bordeaux Dogue is of great interest to all but especially to fanciers of the Bullmastiff. The great similarity in appearance between these two breeds is often brought to light, and Bullmastiff enthusiasts often raise the question as to which of these dogs came into being first. For many reasons, this is really a meaningless question, but, if pressed for an answer to it, that answer can only be that the current form of the Dogue de Bordeaux has been in existence far longer than that of the Bullmastiff. In fact, long before the earliest experiments which were to give rise to the modern-day Bullmastiff breed, the Bordeaux Dogue was already a fine purebred that was clearly recognizable by today's show standards. If to say that the similarity between these two breeds suggests a patriarchal relationship

This fine and ancient breed from France is being brought to us by Steve and Wendy Norris, among others.

between them, then it is clear that the Dogue de Bordeaux must be the father of the Bullmastiff. Historical evidence and literature indicate that no patriarchal relationship exists, however, and the similarities between the Bordeaux Dogue and the Bullmastiff are the result of similar breeding experiments conducted at different times.

Just when the Dogue de Bordeaux first appeared in France is one of many subjects that are commonly debated among purebred historians. Personally, I feel that the breed is undoubtedly one expression of the pre-Christian era of Western European mastiffs, such as those found in Italy (the Neapolitan Mastiff) and England (the British Mastiff). In the way that other Western European mastiffs developed regionally specific characteristics as a result of selective breeding practices and the occasional addition of other regional bloodlines, so did the Dogue de Bordeaux. We know that other Western European mastiffs were commonly used as arena gladiators before the time of Christ, and, as such, it could very well be that the early ancestors of the Bordeaux Dogue were also so employed. In any event, like many of the world's real powerhouse breeds, the Bordeaux Dogue

This shot comes to us from a dog show held in France. If you've got the space, this would be some dog to own, wouldn't it?

was selectively bred for centuries into the past purely for its ability to perform well in animal combat events. Like many of the world's other fighting breeds, the Dogue formerly came in two sizes, large (almost 80 pounds) and larger (over 100 pounds). The smaller of these, the Doguin, was used to bait the bull or the ass, while the larger variety was normally employed as a bearbaiter. The smaller variety is virtually non-existent today, and any reference to the Dogue de Bordeaux can generally be assumed to mean the larger variety.

Contests involving the Bordeaux Dogue were more often staged between two Dogues than between a Dogue and another animal. These were fighting dogs, first and foremost, and matches between two good dogs would often draw large crowds of spectators. Like many of the world's fighting breeds, the ears of the Bordeaux Dogue were generally very closely cropped, and the front of the Dogue was often a mass of scars. Some of the names of fighting Bordeaux Dogues of great acclaim a century ago or more are still available in the literature today. There were such dogs as Caporal, a fighting champion of the Pyrenees for a full seven years, Megere, a bitch that was often matched against wolves, bears, and hyenas, and the great champion Hercules, who

was finally killed in a bloody match against a jaguar in San Francisco.

Scattered reports tell of the fighting of Bordeaux Dogues in Europe today, but if these reports are true, the instances of these fights are very rare. The Dogue is now employed primarily as a companion and guard dog, with tremendous man-stopping ability and a

A terrific shot of a Bordeaux head by Isabelle Français. Owner, Robin Marcelle.

great willingness (some criticize that there is often too much willingness) to test its mettle against any man who dares intrude upon its property. Too many false rumors portray the breed as being dangerous to own, due to its aggressive nature and its ability to do bodily harm. I have personally discussed the temperament of these dogs with many owners of this breed in France and elsewhere and, while all agree that the Dogue is a fantastic guardian, in not one instance have I ever heard of a case in which a Dogue displayed aggression toward any member of its human family. These dogs are safe around adults and, when raised with children,

are known to be completely trustworthy around them.

Outside of France, the Bordeaux Dogue is quite rare. A few Dogues are kept in Holland, Belgium, and Germany. There is some fine breeding stock in Berlin today, where the breed has proven itself to be useful as a city pet as well as being very well suited to country life.

Until recently, the future of the Bordeaux Dogue looked fairly bleak, but upon the founding of the "Dogue de Bordeaux Club of America," this picture has changed dramatically. Working very closely with the foremost authorities on the Bordeaux Dogue breed in France (and I

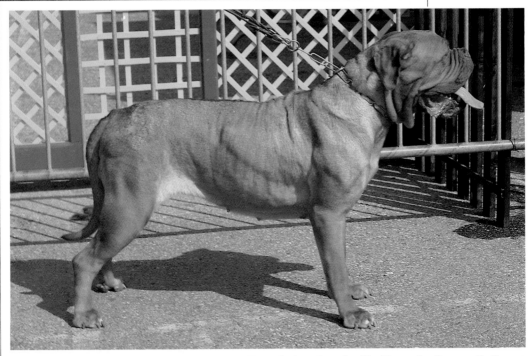

Above: **A grand specimen photographed at a French dog show by Ms. Français. Owner, G. Jeunet.**
Below: **Still knowing his job, the Bordeaux can rest and still be very much "on-duty."**

have checked with the French on this myself), this club has been importing only the finest breeding stock for its own use and has displayed a very cordial willingness to assist others who prefer to import their own Dogues rather than wait for a pup bred at home. Such assistance with importing is very valuable, as the only breeders of Bordeaux Dogues, who have proven to be very interested in exporting pups, have also often proven to export only the worst available.

My advice to anyone who is seriously interested in obtaining a Dogue de Bordeaux is to do so through the breed club and not try to obtain one on your own unless you are very sure that you know what you are doing.

Bear in mind, when purchasing a Bordeaux Dogue, that as long as you have put forth the effort to locate a rare breed and have paid all the money usually charged for any fine purebred, you should insist upon being presented with a member of the breed that is a historically accurate, true representative of what the dogs originally looked like. Too many modern Bordeaux Dogues clearly display evidence of having been constructed, using either Mastiff or Bullmastiff admixture. The red mask is more typical of the Bordeaux Dogue than is the black mask. The red coat is more typical than the fawn coat. A light-colored nose and light-colored eyes, rather than dark, are typical. The Bordeaux Dogue should display a clearly undershot bite. Select for these features, among others, and you will be buying a Bordeaux Dogue rather than a Mastiff or a Bullmastiff.

Once again, the Bordeaux Dogue has proven itself to be an excellent guard dog that has been ignored for too long. Its great strength, combined with its considerable size (a good male will weigh 120 pounds and sometimes more than 150 pounds), assures that it is

This is a fine Dogue de Bordeaux.

always an effective man-stopper. Its surly face denotes its somewhat less than sociable disposition, and this face is situated at the front of the largest head in the world of dogs. With such an enormous selection of homes to burglarize, why would any would-be intruder select a home containing a Dogue de Bordeaux?

Standard for the Dogue de Bordeaux

GENERAL APPEARANCE—This is not a giant among dogs, but he is a massive animal, well built though rather low in stature, very muscular and well balanced overall. The huge head, furrowed by wrinkles, is typical of the

An eye-catching, man-stopping mastiff, who is undeniably massive. Owner, John Blackwell.

The Dogue de Bordeaux boasts the largest head in all dogdom.

breed. The muzzle is square, truncated and short, with a black or red mask. The general appearance is that of an athlete demanding and getting respect—compact, muscular and proud.

SIZE—Weight: for the larger variety called Dogues, males over 100 pounds; females 88 pounds; for the medium variety called Doguins, males 84–100 pounds, females 77–88 pounds. Height at withers: males 23–26 inches; females proportionately smaller.

HEAD—Tremendous, with a characteristic expression and appearance. The skull is broad and short, and its circumference is approximately the same as the height at the withers in males. The stop is abrupt, forming a right angle; the medial furrow is deep. The muzzle is large, short and slightly hollowed; it is square, with prominent cheeks, which are well developed and have an under structure of heavy bone encased in muscle. The jaws are very powerful, broad and square. The lower jaw is undershot by well over ¼ inch. The teeth are very strong, especially the canines, which are only slightly curved. The nose is broad, dark in those dogs with a dark mask, lighter in those with a reddish mask. It is vertical or slightly regressive when the head is held horizontally.

Eyes—Oval, set as far apart as possible, large, not bulging; the supraorbital ridges are pronounced.

Ears—Small and hanging, the front of the ear base is slightly raised. The ears are a little darker than the rest of the coat and slightly rounded at the tips.

NECK—Very strong and muscular, quite robust at the juncture with the shoulders.

BODY—The chest is powerful, broad, deep, let down below the elbows. The circumference of the body behind the elbows should be 10–12 inches more than the height at the withers. The ribs are solid and well sprung. The back is broad and muscular. The loins are short. The withers are high enough to dominate the dorsal line, which should be straight from the beginning to end. The croup should not be rounded or raised but sloping evenly to the point of insertion of the tail.

TAIL—Thick at the root, not reaching farther than the hocks, carried low. It is deeply set on without flag or rough hair below. When the dog is excited, the tail stands at a right angle to normal.

FOREQUARTERS—The shoulders are well sloped, protruding slightly from the withers. Together with the forelegs they form an angle slightly more than 90 degrees. The legs are heavy, exceptionally muscular, vertical, although in particularly broad-chested dogs they are slightly sloped from top to bottom and from inside outward.

HINDQUARTERS— Elongated, with thighs well let down and muscular. The hocks are short and angulated. The hindquarters are not as broad as the forequarters.

FEET—Strong with closed toes and regularly separated nails.

COAT—Fine, short and soft.

Color—Mahogany, fawn, golden, black-speckled. A solid-colored dark coat with warm tones is most desirable. A definite red or black mask is required. Limited black markings are acceptable.

FAULTS—Small head, not in good proportion to the height; long, narrow, Great Dane head; absence of medial furrow; total lack of wrinkles; narrow nose; flesh-colored or mottled nose; nose color contrasting with coat; narrow, pointed, excessively projected or excessively recessed muzzle; Roman nose; soft, bony or underdeveloped cheeks; overshot or not properly undershot jaws; teeth visible, yellow, decayed, badly set, or underdeveloped; lack of stop; small, round eyes, too deep-set, too light, too close, vicious, blind or wall-eyes; conjunctivitis; ears set low, long ears, excessively thick ear cartilage; prick ears, ears carried forward, pointed, shell ears; long or weak neck, flat ribs; undersized false ribs; saddleback, flat back, narrow or weak back; falling belly, paunchy or excessively drawn-up belly; tail too long, trumpet tail, tufted tail; knotty or sinuous tail; lack of tail, even if accidental; weak shoulder, badly muscled shoulders; shoulders too short, straight or flat; elbow turned outward or inward; weak forearm; pasterns turned excessively outward; harefeet, splayed feet; white nails in dark dogs; weak thighs, flat thighs; hocks too straight, causing elevated croup; hocks turned outward or inward; dewclaws; white hair on muzzle; entirely white coat (white is acceptable on chest and feet); heavy, harsh, curly, wavy, excessively long hair; dull coat.

To my mind, this is one heck of a face to be looking into: imagine trying to reason with him if he was mad. Owner, G. Jeunet.

THE FILA BRASILEIRO

Let me inform you that in its own simple way, this is one of the most difficult chapters I've had to write for this book. The first simple reason for the difficulty is that reliable information, at first, was hard to come by—then, after giving up on my American sources and establishing reliable contacts in Brazil, so much reliable information came to me that it was difficult to whittle it all down to one concise chapter written for the average dog enthusiast as opposed to the fanatic. This problem also presented itself in each of the

A strong, well-put-together brindle Fila Brasileiro. Owner, Eduardo Benito Ruiz.

other chapters devoted to the very rare breeds.

The second reason for the difficulty was that the quality of Filas being imported into the U.S.A has changed drastically in only a few short years. A great reputation for quality preceded the breed to the

Finally, however, some better breeding stock began to make its way into the U.S. show ring, and, in the course of three years or so, the general quality of the breed improved almost beyond recognition.

I got myself into serious trouble once with a very large

U.S.A. This early reputation was totally unfounded, as the earliest dogs present were of embarrassing quality. When the first representatives of the breed began to make their way to the rare-breed show ring, they were a tremendous disappointment.

segment of the rare breed enthusiasts on the East Coast (where I live). I let information slip out in print to the general public that the earliest representatives of the breed in the U.S.A. were for the most part pathetic. The trouble seemed so serious to them that the only thing that saved me was that I couldn't care less about any of the people who had decided that I was their mortal enemy—nor could I care less about their attitude, which seemed to suggest that I was destroying their chance to cash in by selling expensive puppies of terrible breeding to unsuspecting rare breed enthusiasts. As I have always felt that there was no room at

all for the profit motivated among purebred dog hobbyists, I was more than happy to play my part in forcing them to improve the quality of their animals.

One argument that a breeder of the then-poor Fila dogs gave me did have enough merit to warrant mention, however. The breeder began a conversation by telling me that in his/her opinion I had set back the Fila

The Great Int. Ch. Camburi do Embirema, owned by Clelia Kruel of Camping Kennel.

Top:
Notice that the ears of these Brazilian Filas have been cropped to indicate that they are working dogs.

Bottom:
This Fila Brasileiro is owned by Eduardo Benito Ruiz.

breed in the U.S.A. possibly ten years in the best case scenario, and at worst I had destroyed the breed's chances of ever gaining popularity in the U.S. (which turned out to be nonsense, by the way). This breeder added, however, "How do you expect us to ever improve the quality of the breed if we can't sell the first few litters of puppies we produce?"

The breeder had a point. You need something to work with before you perfect a breed. You can't afford simply to neuter and give away all those poor quality puppies, because you paid a fortune for the parents yourself. But my arguments are twofold. First, import better stock in the first place and don't begin your program until you have something meaningful to work with. Second, because you have some long-term plan that may make good sense, it doesn't mean that the average person, who has read so many good things about a breed and who is spending his hard-earned money to buy himself something very specific that he wants and believes in, should contribute to your cause by being fooled into buying something he will ultimately be unhappy with.

Should the reader find

No dog can mirror perfectly the breed standard, though Int. Ch. Camburi do Embirema is a force to be reckoned with. Not even owner Clelia Kruel dare tell Camburi that he's not perfect!

himself really getting interested in dogs, let me warn him that the first thing he will learn about the hobby is that most of the people involved have long since forgotten that we are talking about puppies. This is not rocket science, folks, nor is it big business.

Fortunately, a few very well-intending and knowledgeable Brazilian Fila enthusiasts decided that it was great fun that Americans and especially Germans had become interested in their dogs. With their help and with some well-directed effort on the part of a number of American Fila enthusiasts, the quality of the breed has changed dramatically for the

This Fila pup demonstrates the huge bone that is typical of the breed. Owner, Procopio do Valla.

better. The U.S.A. now has a Fila that not only is well put together physically, but also is well suited for serious protection work. While its original "super dog" reputation was a farce, to say that the Fila can be among the best is saying quite a bit.

The history of the Fila is an especially interesting one by way of an introduction to the breed. It will be useful to draw a comparison between the Fila and the Bullmastiff. This is not to imply that the Bullmastiff and the Fila look at all alike or are suitable to the same living conditions; rather, blood is shared between these two breeds, and the purpose for which each breed was originally developed are strikingly similar. As the Bullmastiff was constructed using 60% mastiff and 40% bull stock, the Fila was constructed using similar component breeds.

Spanish and Portuguese conquistadors originally brought the Bloodhound, the Mastiff, and Spanish Bulldog to Brazil; it was these breeds that were used in the development of the Fila. The composition of the Fila is largely a cross between the mastiff and the Bloodhound, with old Spanish Bulldog crossed into this combination to increase the breed's tenacity. It is important to remember that the bulldog used in this cross probably bore no similarity to the modern show-type Bulldog of today; rather, it was probably the bulldog of the old Spanish and

Portuguese type (Perro de Presa and Perro do Presa). Even today, the Spanish Bulldog is a very large (100 pound plus), comparatively ferocious breed that remains quite functionally capable. In these respects, it is entirely different from today's show Bulldog.

Another similarity between the Fila and the Bullmastiff is that each was originally developed to chase, attack, bring down, and hold a man—supposedly without mauling him. At this task, both breeds proved very capable. In the case of the Fila, the dog's specific task was to hunt down, catch, and hold runaway slaves. The heavy Bloodhound infusion was obviously intended to aid the dog in its tracking of slaves.

In viewing a Fila, the breed's ancestry is very apparent. The body is that of a small mastiff, except that its general appearance is very athletic. The head and face tell one

A very typical Fila head. Owner, Emir do Camping.

immediately that the breed comes in part from the Bloodhound, although the "dead on its feet" look that many do not care for in a Bloodhound is absent. This is an obviously powerful, athletic, energetic and yet subdued animal that is well suited for indoor living, in spite of its fairly large size.

Although I have seen many Filas and spoken to many owners and breeders in the U.S.A., Brazil, and Europe, I have never owned a Fila or had a friend who owned one that I could visit frequently and know well. As a result, the

information I am offering here on temperament is secondhand. Considering that we have yet to come to the end of the era of the hugely inflated Fila reputation, I would have preferred to offer information based upon personal knowledge. However, I do think that I have sorted out the reliable from the unreliable information over the past few years and that my observation of these dogs has given me what I believe to be clear impressions.

A well-bred Fila is a calm and steady dog that remains alert at all times and is both capable and willing to spring into action in an instant, should it become necessary to do so. The breed is not inclined to stray but prefers its master's side at all times. Contrary to what one will hear elsewhere about the breed, serious shyness does exist, as it exists within all breeds. While it will occasionally express itself, it is by no means characteristic of the breed. These dogs are selected on the basis of their courage before all else, and a good Fila is a fearless and devoted dog. The Germans have long since demonstrated that these dogs work very well in protection training. However, it was the working dog enthusiasts of Germany, rather than the Brazilians, who originally gave rise to the foolish "super dog" reputation that preceded the breed to the U.S.A. The breed is world renowned for its acceptance of children as members of its family. I have never heard of any problem arising between a Fila and a child.

To the surprise of the many American Fila breeders who undoubtedly thought that I was out to get them a few years ago, I would recommend these dogs highly for anyone in search of a trainable, naturally inclined, guard/protection dog. Find yourself a good Fila and you have found yourself a devoted friend that will protect you with its life should it ever be called upon to do so. As with any breed, one should only purchase a pup after personally seeing its parentage and visiting

A good Fila passing the day at a rare breed show.

The Fila "is always docile toward its owner and is extremely tolerant of children."

a few kennels. If, after that, you decide you might like to obtain a pup from foreign sources, you are in luck. Those Brazilian breeders who have been most actively campaigning the breed are, in my experience, honest, reliable, genuine purebred enthusiasts who campaign for the love of the sport alone. Isn't it nice to meet people like that?

Standard for the Fila Brasileiro

GENERAL APPEARANCE—Typical mastiff type dog. Powerful bone, rectangular structure, compact but harmonic and proportionate. Very agile. Courage, determination, and outstanding bravery are the essence of this breed's character. Its faithfulness is proverbial. The disposition of the breed is generally calm, but when called into action, it becomes very aggressive. It is always docile toward its owner and is extremely tolerant of children.

SIZE—Height: males 27–29½ inches; bitches 24–27½ inches. Weight: Males minimum of 110 pounds; bitches minimum 90 pounds.

GAIT—Long, reaching, and elastic gait. The main characteristic of its movement is the pace, which is a two beat lateral gait in which the legs on each side move back and forth as a pair, causing a rolling or rocking motion of the body,

HEAD—Even in proportion to the large body of the dog, the head is big, heavy, and massive.

Stop—Very slight stop.

Muzzle—Strong, broad, and deep. The upper lips are thick and pendulous and hang over the lower lips.

Eyes—From medium to large size, almond shaped, spaced well apart in medium to deep set. Permissible colors are from dark brown to yellow, always in accordance with the coat color.

NECK—Extraordinarily strong and muscled. Dewlap at the throat.

TOPLINE—Withers set well apart from one another. The croup is higher than the withers.

BODY—Strong, broad, and deep. Covered by a thick and loose skin.

LOWERLINE—A long chest that is parallel to the ground. Tucked up slightly but never "Whippetish."

FORELEGS—Strong bone. Legs parallel and straight to the pasterns.

HIND LEGS—Parallel. Strong tarsus, metatarsus slightly bent, higher than the metacarpus. Moderately angled stifle and metatarsus.

TAIL—Very thick at the root. Medium set, tapering rapidly as it reaches the hocks.

COLOR—All solid colors are permitted except all white, mouse gray, coat with patches or spotted marks. Brindles with a solid coat may have stripes with less intensity or very strong dark stripes. A black mask may or may not be present. In all colors, white marks are allowed on feet, chest, and tip of tail. White marks are not desirable on any other part of the body.

SKIN—One of the most important characteristics is the thick, loose skin all over the body and chiefly at the neck forming a pronounced dewlap. Many times it can be seen at the brisket or abdomen. Some individuals present folds on the side of the head and also at the withers running down the shoulders.

COAT—Short, smooth, dense, and tight to the body.

TEMPERAMENT—A standard temperament test, included in all judgings of the Fila in Brazil, includes being attacked by a man with a stick, and a shooting test. The dog should display courage, determination, and a dislike of strangers. The dog should always be self-assured.

A young male Fila displaying an interesting brindle coat pattern.

THE GERMAN SHEPHERD DOG

Above: The GSD is one of the world's most trainable animals. Owner, Liv McLea.

So as not to turn anyone off right at the start of this section, let me begin by saying that some of the most intelligent, most discriminating, most faithful, and most capable of all guard dogs have been and are German Shepherd Dogs. Now, let me tell you that I came within a hair of not discussing this breed at all. Why the discrepancy? Due to the early recognition of this breed as a fine working dog, the breed

A good German Shepherd can be among the most athletic of dogs; it is ironic that the breed's numbers suffer from hip dysplasia. Potential owners should insist that their dogs are certified to be "HD-excellent."

became so popular throughout the world (especially the United States) that widespread, alarmingly inept breeding practices reduced the quality of the German Shepherd Dog in general. As a result, the average German Shepherd Dog today may not be suited, either physically or temperamentally, for duty as a reliable and effective guard dog.

The breed name "German Shepherd" has almost become a generic term among the lay public for poorly bred dogs of an approximate German Shepherd physical type. Many of the dogs casually referred to as German Shepherds are not even purebred animals, while many others may qualify for registry papers but are hardly well-bred dogs. Temperamental problems, especially shyness

and hyperactivity, are common among these dogs. Physical problems such as hip malformation (dysplasia) are more common among "Shepherds" than among any other breed.

Some knowledgeable German Shepherd Dog enthusiasts are of the opinion that the overall quality of German-born puppies is better than the overall quality of these dogs elsewhere, and to have your dealer import a German Shepherd pup is to ensure that you will receive a quality dog. In my opinion, this is not the case. Some fine show and working German Shepherds (the British sometimes call these dogs Alsatians, by the way) are produced elsewhere today. Mailing your money off to any German breeder is by no means a guarantee that you will be buying a well-bred dog.

My advice to anyone who is serious about obtaining a really well-bred German Shepherd Dog would be to buy a locally bred dog. With much less effort than will be required to secure a dog through foreign contacts, you can probably locate a fine dog close to home. The place to start your search is at the library of your national breed registry. Ask for information on the location of a local breed club, contact the club for a listing of reliable breeders, and purchase your pup from a reliable breeder. When it comes time to make a purchase, be prepared to part with a good deal more money than the guy in your local junkyard will want for his pup. Stay away from the very large breeding stock, as a 130-pound

A well-bred German Shepherd can turn anyone's head when he's "set up" for a judging or for a photograph. This is Ch. Covy's Tarragon of Tucker Hill owned by Gloria Birch, J. Stevens, and Cappy Pottle. The judge is Ernest H. Hart.

German Shepherd Dog is the most likely candidate in the world of dogs for serious hip trouble. Ask to see some of the older dogs in your pup's background and observe their movement carefully for any evidence of limping. Insist upon O.F.A. certification of as many of your dog's ancestors as possible. Such certification can help to ensure that your dog's hips will develop normally and that no crippling problems will arise as the dog matures.

On a more positive note, if you have done your homework and selected your German Shepherd Dog carefully, you will soon understand why so many members of this breed are named "King" and "Duke." This is truly a royal animal that epitomizes what a useful guard dog should be. It is an incredibly handsome dog, a super intelligent dog, a fine athlete among dogs, a devoted protector and family pet, possessing enough power and courage to stop a man in his tracks should the need to do so ever arise.

The German Shepherd Dog has excelled not only as a pet and guard dog, a police and military dog, but also as a guide dog for the blind. As the breed name implies, it began its career as a shepherd's dog and can still be used effectively as such.

The breed was originally produced using the various shepherd dog breeding stock that was indigenous throughout Germany. Due to what some view as its "wolf-like" appearance, it has been speculated that the modern

Shepherd.

German Shepherd Dog was composed by crossing local shepherd dogs to local wolves, but this is highly unlikely.

The first German Shepherd Dog club was formed in Germany in 1899, and the development of the modern German Shepherd Dog has progressed since that time. Its current show form is, then, a relatively recent development, but one which is very highly regarded throughout the world.

Once again, employing any strategy other than the utmost caution is a big mistake in the selection of a German Shepherd puppy. Know these dogs well before you buy, and never buy a German Shepherd Dog on impulse or because you have been offered a good price.

As good a choice for a family guard dog as a well-bred German Shepherd can be, I must end this section on a note of discouragement. Unless you are really prepared to investigate your breed and its

breeders very carefully prior to buying your puppy, selecting this breed is probably the worst choice you could make from among the breeds discussed in this book. Remember the definition of a useful guardian breed: a high percentage of individuals from among the breed are useful as guard dogs. As paradoxical as this may sound, that high percentage of useful guardians no longer defines the German Shepherd Dog breed.

Standard for the German Shepherd Dog

GENERAL APPEARANCE—The first impression of a good German Shepherd Dog is that of a strong, agile, well-muscled animal, alert and full of life. It is well balanced, with harmonious development of the forequarter and hindquarter. The dog is longer than tall, deep bodied, and presents an outline of smooth curves rather than angles. It looks substantial and not spindly, giving the impression, both at rest and in motion, of muscular fitness and nimbleness, without any look of clumsiness or soft living. The ideal dog is stamped with a look of quality and nobility— difficult to define but unmistakable when present. Secondary sex characteristics

Opposite: The protective instincts of a breed of dog are transferable from the parent–puppy bond to the dog–human bond. That a dog makes a reliable parent can be a plus for a guard dog. Owner, Louise Morneau.

Right: A trio of German Shepherds. The breed is known for its gregarious nature.

The German Shepherd is a renowned athlete. Not all members of the breed will take to the water as ardently as this one, but if you acquire one who will, your every pool party is sure to be a splash!

are strongly marked, and every animal gives a definite impression of masculinity or femininity according to its sex.

CHARACTER—The breed has a distinct personality marked by direct and fearless but not hostile expression, self-confidence and a certain aloofness that does not lend itself to immediate and indiscriminate friendships. The dog must be approachable, quietly standing its ground and showing confidence and willingness to meet overtures without making them itself. It is poised, but when the occasion demands, eager and alert; both fit and willing to serve in its capacity as companion, watchdog, blind leader, herding dog, or guardian, whichever the circumstances may demand. The dog must not be timid, shrinking behind its master or handler; it should not be nervous, looking about or upward with anxious expression or showing nervous reactions, such as tucking of tail, to strange sights or sounds. Lack of confidence under any surroundings is not typical of good character. Any of the above deficiencies in character which indicate shyness must be penalized as very serious faults and any dog exhibiting pronounced indications of these must be excused from the ring. It must be possible for the judge to observe the teeth and to determine if both testicles have descended. Any dog that attempts to bite the judge must be disqualified. The ideal dog is a working animal with an incorruptible character combined with the body and gait suitable for the arduous work that constitutes its primary purpose.

HEAD—The head is noble, cleanly chiseled, strong without coarseness, but above all, not fine, and in proportion to the body. The head of the male is distinctly masculine and that of the bitch distinctly feminine. The muzzle is long and strong with the lips firmly fitted, and its topline is parallel to the topline of the skull. Seen from the front, the forehead is only moderately arched, and the skull slopes into the long, wedge-shaped muzzle without abrupt stop. Jaws are strongly developed.

Ears—Ears are moderately pointed, in proportion to the skull, open toward the front, and carried erect when at attention, the ideal carriage being one in which the center lines of the ears, viewed from the front, are parallel to each other and perpendicular to the ground. A dog with cropped or hanging ears must be disqualified.

Eyes—Of medium size, almond shaped, set a little

A classic photo of three German Shepherd Dogs.

obliquely and not protruding. The color is as dark as possible. The expression keen, intelligent, and composed.

Teeth—42 in number—20 upper and 22 lower—are strongly developed and meet in a scissors bite in which part of the inner surface of the upper incisors meet and engage part of the outer surface of the lower incisors. An overshot jaw or a level bite is undesirable. An undershot jaw is a disqualifying fault. Complete dentition is to be preferred. Any missing teeth other than first premolars is a serious fault.

NECK—The neck is strong and muscular, clean-cut and relatively long, proportionate in size to the head and without loose folds of skin. When the dog is at attention or excited, the head is raised and the neck carried high; otherwise typical carriage of the head is forward rather than up and but a little higher than the top of the shoulders, particularly in motion.

FOREQUARTERS—The shoulder blades are long and obliquely angled, laid on flat and not placed forward. The upper arm joins the shoulder blade at about a right angle. Both the upper arm and the shoulder blade are well muscled. The forelegs viewed from all sides are straight and the bone oval rather than round. The pasterns are strong and springy and angulated at approximately a 25-degree angle from the vertical.

FEET—The feet are short, compact, with toes well arched, pads thick and firm, nails short and dark. The dewclaws, if any, should be removed from the hind legs. Dewclaws on the forelegs may be removed, but are normally left on.

PROPORTION—The German Shepherd Dog is longer than tall, with the most desirable proportion as 10 to 8½. The desired height for males at top of the highest point of the shoulder blade is 24–26 inches; and for bitches 22–24 inches. The length is measured from the point of the prosternum or breastbone to the rear edge of the pelvis, the ischial tuberosity.

BODY—The whole structure of the body gives an impression of depth and solidity without bulkiness.

Chest—Commencing at the prosternum, it is well filled and carried well down between the legs. It is deep and capacious, never shallow, with ample room for lungs and heart, carried well forward, with the prosternum showing ahead of the shoulder in profile.

Ribs—Well sprung and long, neither barrel shaped nor too flat, carried down

to a sternum which reaches to the elbows. Correct ribbing allows the elbows to move back freely when the dog is at a trot. Too round causes interference and throws the elbows out; too flat or too short causes pinched elbows. Ribbing is carried well back so that the loin is relatively short. *Abdomen*—Firmly held and not paunchy. The bottom line is only moderately tucked up in the loin.

TOPLINE—

Withers—The withers are high and slope into the level back.

Back—The back is straight, very strongly developed without sag or roach, and relatively short. The desirable long proportion

Attentive and intelligent, the GSD enjoys one of the largest purebred fancies in the United States. Do not chose your dog hastily; not every breeder is producing acceptable representatives of the breed. A bad Shepherd is sure to be a heartbreaking experience; good Shepherds, animals the quality of these two, will delight their owners beyond expectation. Owners, Jack and Sue Nugent.

is not derived from a long back, but from overall length with relation to height, which is achieved by length of forequarter and length of hindquarter and withers, viewed from the side.

Loin—Viewed from the top, broad and strong. Undue length between the last rib and the thigh, when viewed from the side, is undesirable.

Croup—Long and gradually sloping.

TAIL—Bushy, with the last vertebra extended at least to the hock joint. It is set smoothly into the croup and low rather than high. At rest, the tail hangs in a slight curve like a saber. A slight hook—sometimes carried to one side—is faulty only to the extent that it mars general appearance. When the dog is excited or in motion the curve is accentuatcd and the tail raised, but it should never be curled forward beyond a vertical line. Tails too short, or with clumpy ends due to ankylosis, are serious faults. A dog with a docked tail must be disqualified.

HINDQUARTERS—The whole assembly of the thigh viewed from the side is broad, with both upper and lower thigh well muscled, forming as nearly as possible a right angle. The upper thigh bone parallels the shoulder blade while the lower thigh bone parallels the upper arm. The metatarsus

A lesson in attack training underway. Elli Matlin is the owner of Highland Hills Tarter.

(the unit between the hock joint and the foot) is short, strong and tightly articulated.

GAIT—A German Shepherd Dog is a trotting dog, and its structure has been developed to meet the requirements of its work. The general impression of the gait is outreaching, elastic, seemingly without effort, smooth and rhythmic, covering the maximum amount of ground with the minimum number of steps. At a walk it covers a great deal of ground, with long stride of both hind legs and forelegs. At a trot the dog covers still more ground with even longer stride, and moves powerfully but easily, with co-ordination and balance so that the gait appears to be the steady motion of a well-lubricated machine. The feet travel close to the ground on both forward reach and backward push. In order to achieve ideal movement of this kind, there must be good muscular development and ligamentation. The hindquarters deliver, through the back, a powerful forward thrust which slightly lifts the whole animal and drives the body forward. Reaching far under and passing the imprint left by the front foot, the hind foot takes hold of the ground; then hock, stifle and upper thigh come into play and sweep back, the stroke of the hind leg finishing with the foot still close to the ground in a smooth follow-through. The overreach of the hindquarter usually necessitates one hind foot passing outside and the other hind foot passing inside the track of the forefeet, and such action is not faulty unless the locomotion is crabwise with the dog's body sideways out of the normal straight line.

Transmission—The typical smooth, flowing gait is maintained with great strength and firmness of back. The whole effort of the hindquarter is transmitted to the forequarter through the loin, back, and withers. At full trot the back must remain firm and level without sway, roll, whip or roach. Unlevel topline with the withers lower than the hip is a fault. To compensate for the forward motion imparted by the hindquarters, the shoulder should open to its full extent. The forelegs should reach out close to the ground in a long stride in harmony with that of the hindquarters. The dog does not track on widely separated parallel lines, but brings the feet inward toward the middle line of the body when trotting in order to maintain balance. The feet track closely but do not strike or cross over. Viewed from the front, the front legs function from the shoulder joint to the pad in a straight line. Viewed from the rear, the hind legs function from the hip joint to the pad in a straight line. Faults of gait, whether from front, rear, or side, are to be considered very serious.

COAT—The ideal dog has a double coat of medium length. The outer coat should be as dense as possible, hair straight, harsh and lying close to the body. A slightly wavy outer coat, often of wiry texture, is permissible. The head, including the inner ear and foreface, and the legs and paws are covered with short hair, and the neck with longer and thicker hair. The rear of the forelegs and hind legs has somewhat longer hair extending to the pastern and hock respectively. Faults in coat include soft, silky, too long outer coat, woolly, curly, and open coat.

Color—The German Shepherd Dog varies in color, and most colors are permissible. Strong rich colors are preferred. Nose black. Pale, washed-out colors and blues or livers are serious faults. A white dog or a dog with a nose that is not predominantly black must be disqualified.

Solid black Shepherds are less common than black and tan ones; for some these dogs are even more striking. They can, however, be easily mistaken for the Belgian Sheepdog (Malinois) by the novice. Owners, Shirley and David Panijan.

GERMAN SHEPHERD DOG
CLUB OF DETROIT
MAY 31, 1981
JUDGE — B. AMIDON
BEST OF BREED

PHOTO — TOM MONAHAN

THE GIANT SCHNAUZER

Opposite: **A much more serious guardian breed than many people realize, the Giant Schnauzer can be among the best of the best.**

Left: **A Giant "stacked" to reveal a sturdy, demanding conformation. Photo by Isabelle Français. Owner, Carol Thordsen.**

Few breeds have impressed me upon first sight as much as the Giant Schnauzer. I remember the first time I ever saw a Giant Schnauzer as clearly as if it were yesterday. I had walked into a local ice cream parlor, leaned myself up against a high counter, ordered one form of ice cream or another, and, while it was being made up, played with the money that I had readily available for the payment of the ice cream. The money slipped out of my hands and dropped down on an ice cream bin on the opposite side of the counter. Without thinking or looking, I leaned over the counter and reached for the bill. Suddenly I heard a who had calmed the dog, I not only learned that the dog was a very carefully bred Giant Schnauzer that had been imported as a pup to the United States from Germany, but I also learned that this man

A Giant being used for attack work. Trust me! If you've ever seen one of these dogs go, you'll never want one mad at you. This photo was snapped in the Fatherland, Germany.

thunderous growl emanate from what at first registered in my mind as being a large, black, bearskin rug. One word from the ice cream parlor owner was uttered to the dog in German and it became silent, but it watched me suspiciously out of the corner of its eye as I picked up my money.

Upon questioning the somewhat elderly German man

was a serious breeder of "Giants" or, as they are called in Germany, the Reisenschnauzer and that there was nothing he liked better than talking about dogs and showing off the lengthy book of show pictures that he always had within reach. A young woman took over the counter as I got my first lesson on Schnauzer dogs.

Germany produces three varieties of Schnauzer: the Miniature Schnauzer, the Standard Schnauzer, and the Giant Schnauzer. It should be clear, at the onset of your consideration of a Giant as a guard dog, that a Giant is not just an over-sized Standard Schnauzer. The Giant was produced using very different bloodlines than the Standard Schnauzer, and it is a relatively new addition as a purebred by comparison as well.

Originally developed in Southern Bavaria at the end of the nineteenth century, the Giant Schnauzer was produced by crossing such breeds as the local smooth-coated drover dogs, local rough-coated shepherd dogs, the black Great Dane, and possibly the Bouvier. In the early days of the breed, its primary function was that of a great cattle dog, and it was really not until World War I that the breed gained recognition outside of Bavaria for its exceptional ability as a police and guard dog.

Giant Schnauzers were first

Somewhat different in appearance than many of the guardian breeds, the Giant Schnauzer offers a great alternative to the other man-stoppers. Owner, Carol Thordsen.

imported to the United States in 1925 and first recognized by the AKC in 1930. The breed has achieved considerable gains in popularity among American purebred enthusiasts since that time, but it has never really achieved the level of popularity that one would expect of such a loyal, intelligent, and capable family and working dog.

Perhaps it is the association between the Giant Schnauzer and the smaller varieties of Schnauzers that causes many dog enthusiasts to underestimate the ability of the Giant as an effective man-stopping guard dog. In no uncertain terms, let me assure you that the Giant is an extremely intelligent, fast moving, quick thinking, very discriminating, very willing, powerful animal. Many of the world's greatest attack trainers will tell you that the Giant has

no less hitting power than does a good Rottweiler. In case you have never seen a Rottweiler hit, I attest that this is saying a great deal about the ability of a Giant Schnauzer to bring down a man. This is a breed of powerful body and powerful bite. While an intruder may fight for his life against a strong Giant Schnauzer, this is a dog that can inflict serious injury upon a man in a short period of time. These are the qualities that distinguish the average watchdog from a true guardian.

Like its cousin the Bouvier, the Giant Schnauzer is a very steady dog around its human family, and it has proven its worth as a guide dog for the blind as well. While it is an active dog that will require quite a bit of exercise, it is not of a hyperactive nature and, as such, in spite of its size, it is perfectly suitable as an indoor

The Giant Schnauzer is a clean and easy dog to own. If you're inclined to own two guard dogs, consider a pair of Giants. Owner, Beth Carlson.

dog and even as a dog for a large apartment. Give the Giant Schnauzer some serious consideration in your shopping for a guard dog.

Standard for the Giant Schnauzer

GENERAL APPEARANCE—The Giant Schnauzer should resemble, as nearly as possible, in general appearance, a larger and more powerful version of the Standard Schnauzer, on the whole a bold and valiant figure of a dog. Robust, strongly built, nearly square in proportion of body length to height at withers, active, sturdy, and well muscled. Temperament which combines spirit and alertness with intelligence and reliability. Composed, watchful, courageous, easily trained, deeply loyal to family, playful, amiable in repose, and a commanding figure when aroused. The sound, reliable temperament, rugged build, and dense weather-resistant wiry coat make for one of the most useful, powerful, and enduring working breeds.

HEAD—Strong, rectangular in appearance, and elongated; narrowing slightly from the ears to the eyes, and again from the eyes to the tip of the nose. The total length

of the head is about one-half the length of the back (withers to set-on of tail). The head matches the sex and substance of the dog. The topline of the muzzle is parallel to the topline of the skull; there is a slight stop which is accentuated by the eyebrows.

Skull—(Occiput to Stop). Moderately broad between the ears; occiput not too prominent. Top of skull flat; skin unwrinkled.

Cheeks—Flat, but with well-developed chewing muscles; there is no "cheekiness" to disturb the rectangular head appearance (with beard).

Muzzle—Strong and well filled under the eyes; both parallel and equal in length to the topskull; ending in a moderately blunt wedge. The nose is large, black and full. The lips are tight, and not overlapping, black in color.

Bite—A full complement of sound white teeth (6/6 incisors, 2/2 canines, 8/8 premolars, 4/6 molars) with a scissors bite. The upper and lower jaws are powerful and well formed. **Disqualifying Faults—** Overshot or undershot.

Ears—When cropped, identical in shape and length with pointed tips. They are in balance with the head and not

Cropping the Schnauzer's ears gives it a sharper appearance; uncropped Giants have a more sedate, restful look to them. Photo by Isabelle Français. Courtesy of Gallantry Giant Schnauzers: Ben Bleckley, Herb Newborg, and Ron and Lisa Gamone.

THE GIANT SCHNAUZER

The Giant's neck is well arched and strong. Owner, Linda Strydio.

exaggerated in length. They are set high on the skull and carried perpendicularly at the inner edges with as little bell as possible along the other edges. When uncropped, the ears are V-shaped button ears of medium length and

thickness, set high and carried rather high and close to the head.

Eyes—Medium size, dark brown, and deep-set. They are oval in appearance and keen in expression with lids fitting tightly. Vision shoulders, and with skin fitting tightly at the throat; in harmony with the dog's weight and build.

BODY—Compact, substantial, short-coupled, and strong, with great power and agility. The height at the highest

The breed's body is described as compact and substantial. Photo by Isabelle Français. Owner, Carol Thordsen.

is not impaired nor eyes hidden by too long eyebrows.

NECK—Strong and well arched, of moderate length, blending cleanly into the point of the withers equals the body length from breastbone to point of rump. The loin section is well developed, as short as possible for compact build.

Can you see yourself in this picture walking your Giant? I know I can.

FOREQUARTERS—The forequarters have flat, somewhat sloping shoulders and high withers. Forelegs are straight and vertical when viewed from all sides with strong pasterns and good bone. They are separated by a fairly deep brisket which precludes a pinched front. The elbows are set close to the body and point directly backwards.

Chest—Medium in width, ribs well sprung but with no tendency toward a barrel chest; oval in cross section; deep through the brisket. The breastbone is plainly discernible, with strong forechest; the brisket descends at least to the elbows, and ascends gradually toward the rear with the belly moderately drawn up. The ribs spread gradually from the first rib so as to allow space for the elbows to move close to the body.

Shoulders—The sloping shoulder blades (scapulae) are strongly muscled, yet flat. They are well laid back so that from the side the rounded upper ends are in a nearly vertical line above the elbows, slope well forward to the point where they join the upper arm (humerus), forming as nearly as possible a right angle.

Such an angulation permits the maximum forward extension of the forelegs without binding or effort. Both shoulders and upper arms are long, permitting depth of chest at the brisket.

Back—Short, straight, strong, and firm.

TAIL—The tail is set moderately high and carried high in excitement. It should be docked to the second and not more than the third joint (approximately one-and-one-half to about three inches long at maturity).

HINDQUARTERS—The hindquarters are strongly muscled, in balance with the

Here's a face a person could grow to love, especially when you know how much the dog behind it loves you. Photo by Isabelle Français. Courtesy of Gallantry Giant Schnauzers.

The Giant Schnauzer occurs in two attractive color possibilities: solid black and pepper and salt.

forequarters; upper thighs are slanting and well bent of the stifles, with the second thighs (tibiae) approximately parallel to an extension of the upper neckline. The legs from the hock joint to the feet are short, perpendicular to the ground while the dog is standing naturally, and from the rear parallel to each other. The hindquarters do not appear over-built or higher than the shoulders. Croup full and slightly rounded.

FEET—Well-arched, compact and catlike, turning neither in nor out, with thick tough pads and dark nails.

Dewclaws—Dewclaws, if any, on hind legs should be removed; on the forelegs, may be removed.

GAIT—The trot is the gait at which movement is judged. Free, balanced and vigorous, with good reach in the forequarters and good driving power in the hindquarters. Rear and front legs are thrown neither in nor out. When moving at a fast trot, a properly built dog will single-track. Back remains strong, firm, and flat.

COAT—Hard, wiry, very dense; composed of a soft undercoat and a harsh outer coat which, when seen against the grain, stands slightly up off the back, lying neither smooth nor flat. Coarse hair on top of head; harsh beard and eyebrows, the Schnauzer hallmark.

COLOR—Solid black or pepper and salt.

Black—A truly pure black. A small white spot on the breast is permitted; any other markings are disqualifying faults.

Pepper and Salt—Outer coat of a combination of banded hairs (white with black and black with white) and some black and white hairs, appearing gray from a short distance. *Ideally:* an intensely pigmented medium gray shade with "peppering" evenly distributed throughout the coat, and a gray undercoat. *Acceptable:* all shades of pepper and salt from dark iron-gray to silver-gray. Every shade of coat has a dark facial mask to emphasize the expression; the color of the mask harmonizes with the shade of the body coat. Eyebrows, whiskers, cheeks, throat, chest, legs, and under tail are lighter in color but include "peppering." Markings are disqualifying faults.

HEIGHT—The height of the withers of the male is 25½ to 27½ inches, and of the female 23½ to 25½ inches, with the mediums being desired. Size alone should never take precedence over type, balance, soundness, and temperament. It should be noted that too small dogs generally lack the power and too large dogs, the agility and maneuverability, desired in a working dog.

FAULTS—The foregoing description is that of the ideal Giant Schnauzer. Any deviation from the above described dog must be penalized to the extent of the deviation. The judge shall dismiss from the ring any shy or vicious Giant Schnauzer

Shyness—A dog shall be judged fundamentally shy if, refusing to stand for examination, it repeatedly shrinks away from the judge; if it fears unduly any approach from the rear; if it shies to a marked degree at sudden and unusual noises.

Viciousness—A dog that attacks or attempts to attack either the judge or its handler is definitely vicious. An aggressive or belligerent attitude towards other dogs shall not be deemed viciousness.

DISQUALIFICATIONS—Overshot or undershot. Markings other than specified.

Strong and rectangular in shape, the Schnauzer's head is an impressive sight.

THE
KUVASZ

Here is a beautiful dog that purebred enthusiasts have, for some unknown reason, never become very excited about, and guard dog enthusiasts have just as mysteriously ignored. The lack of enthusiasm about the Kuvasz (plural of Kuvasz is *Kuvaszok*) among purebred and guard dog enthusiasts is unfortunate, as these dogs generally make excellent family pets and companion dogs as well as low-key but willing, fearless, and determined guard dogs. Their great size (up to 29½ inches and over 100 pounds for a large male) combined with this willingness, fearlessness, and determination also make these dogs very effective man-stoppers.

Perhaps what surprises me most about the lack of popularity of the Kuvasz is that this valuable package of

THE KUVASZ

physical and temperamental charactistics is presented in a surprisingly pastoral-looking body style. The Kuvasz is a pure white dog with a very attractive coat and a face that has to endear the breed to anyone who is inclined to like dogs. Around its human family, it is a loyal and docile tail-wagger—just the kind of dog you normally look at and think you would love to own but avoid because you want your dog to work well as a home guardian. But the Kuvasz does work well as a home guardian; in fact, it ranks among the best. In the words of one very sincere and knowledgeable breeder whom I spoke to on this subject recently, "if you own a Kuvasz, you can be sure it's always ready to die for you with no hesitation." My investigation of this breed has taught me that the breeder was correct. The Kuvasz is a terrific dog.

The name "Kuvasz" is probably derived from the Turkish word for guard (*kuwasz*), and it seems that this breed is both a natural guard and somewhat Turkish. Although the Kuvasz is now found in Hungary and is classified as being a Hungarian breed, due to its long history in that country, it is most likely that the Kuvaszok were brought to Hungary by the Kumans. The Kumans were nomadic shepherds of Turkish origin who, during the thirteenth century, retreated to Hungary in flight from Mongol warriors from the east. Many feel that the actual origin of the breed lies in Tibet, however, and that the breed is basically an expression of the Tibetan shepherd dogs. Some maintain that the origin of the Kuvasz lies in Hungary and the breed is essentially of early Hungarian development. In view of the fact that Kuvasz-type dogs are found between Turkey and Hungary, it is highly unlikely that the Hungarian origin of this breed will ever be substantiated.

During the fifteenth century, the Kuvasz was maintained on large estates throughout Hungary and was a favorite of the Royal Court. King Matthias, who reigned at the time, trusted his Kuvasz more than any man and had one of the dogs with him wherever he went.

Kuvaszok were not only used as personal protection dogs in early Hungary but also as large game hunters. Later these dogs were employed as shepherds and were found to be very effective in their performance of this duty.

Today the Kuvasz is known primarily as a companion dog and as a show dog, but those who know the breed realize that its greatest value lies in the area of its abilities as a guard dog. It is a trainable and loyal breed which will display a great preference for its human family and an aloofness around strangers. It is not a good breed to acquire as an adult in many instances, due to the bond it forms with its original family.

When looking for a Kuvasz, look for puppies; choose another breed if you have any doubts about your ability to keep the dog for its entire life.

Anyone who is attracted to the Kuvasz because of its appearance but who would prefer that the breed were either a bit smaller or larger has the option of choosing from two other very physically similar breeds. The smaller of these breeds is known as the Maremma Sheepdog, or the Pastero-Maremmano-Abruzzese of Italy. A smaller Maremma Sheepdog can weigh between 65 and 77 pounds, depending

The Maremma Sheepdog of Italy is similar though smaller than the Hungarian Kuvasz. Those who know this Italian sheep guard virtually never refer to the breed without raising their eyebrows in respect. Owner, Mrs. Myrta Gelpi Allevamento della Fornarina.

Maremma competing in a conformation show.

upon the sex of the animal, while a larger one will range from 88 to 99 pounds. The height is from 25½ to 29 inches for males and 23½ to 27 inches for females. These dogs are very similar to the Kuvasz in appearance and also in temperament. They have an excellent reputation as guard dogs as well as shepherds. The overall look of the dog is such that only the trained eye can distinguish a large member of this breed from a Kuvasz. Unfortunately, these dogs are rather rare, and purchase may involve making foreign contacts.

The Great Pyrenees is a very large breed which has an appearance similar to that of the Kuvasz but not as much as the Maremma Sheepdog. This French breed stands as high as 31½ inches at the withers and can weigh 120 pounds. While the breed is known as an excellent sheepdog, it is not one that I will recommend as a home guardian. Unfortunately, while some Great Pyrenees dogs work well as guards, too many simply do not. As such, selecting a puppy of this breed as a guard can be a disappointing proposition.

Consider the Kuvasz as a family dog and home protector if you prefer the look of this dog to that of some of the others discussed here. It is a wonderful combination of beauty, brains, and brawn.

Standard for the Kuvasz

GENERAL CHARACTERISTICS—

A spirited dog of keen intelligence, determination, courage and curiosity. Very sensitive to praise and blame. Primarily a one-family dog. Devoted, gentle and patient without being overly demonstrative. Always ready to protect loved ones even to the point of self-sacrifice. Extremely strong instinct to protect children. Polite to accepted strangers, but rather suspicious and very discriminating in making new friends. Unexcelled guard, possessing the ability to act on his own initiative at just the right moment, with instruction. Bold, courageous and fearless. Untiring ability to work and cover rough terrain for long periods of time. Has good sense of smell and has been used to hunt game.

APPEARANCE—A working dog of larger size, sturdily built, well balanced, neither lanky nor cobby. White in color with *no markings*. Medium boned, well muscled, without the slightest hint of bulkiness or lethargy. Impresses the eye with strength and activity combined with light-footedness, moves freely on strong legs. Trunk and limbs form a horizontal rectangle slightly deviated from the square. Slightly inclined croup. Hindquarters are particularly well developed. Any tendency to weakness or lack of substance is a decided fault.

GAIT—Easy, free and elastic. Feet travel close to ground. Hind legs reach far under, meeting or even passing the imprints of the front legs. Moving toward an observer, the front legs do not travel parallel to each other but rather close together at the ground. As speed increases, the legs gradually angle more inward until the pads are almost single-tracking. Unless excited, the head is carried rather low at the level of the shoulders. Desired

movement cannot be maintained without sufficient angulation and firm slimness of body.

SIZE—

Height—Measured at the withers: dogs, 28 to 30 inches; bitches, 26 to 28 inches.

Weight—Dogs, approximately 100 to 115 pounds; bitches, approximately 70 to 90 pounds.

HEAD—Proportions are of great importance as the head

An adolescent Kuvasz. The rate of maturation of a breed is a worthwhile consideration for the potential owner. Owner, Nola Stevens.

is considered to be the most beautiful part of the Kuvasz. Length of head measured from tip of nose to occiput is slightly less than half the height of the dog at the withers. Width is half the length of the head. The skull is elongated but not pointed. The stop is defined, never abrupt, raising the forehead gently above the plane of the muzzle. The longitudinal midline of the forehead is pronounced, widening as it slopes to the muzzle. Cheeks flat, bony arches above the eyes. The skin is dry, no excess flews.

Muzzle—Length in proportion to the length of the head, top straight, not pointed, underjaw well developed. Inside of the

Originally described to me as "a dog that will die for you," the Kuvasz is also a breed that should be considered for house and family protection. Owner, Joseph A. Zielinski.

While the number of Kuvaszok in the show ring is hardly considerable, the Maremma Sheepdog has yet to turn the head of an A.K.C. judge. It is a phenomenon of the modern-day show world why both these outstanding, talented and beautiful canines have been so overlooked.

mouth is preferably black.

Nose—Large, black nostrils well opened.

Lips—Black, closely covering teeth. The upper lip covers the upper jaw only. Lower lip tight and not pendulous.

Bite—Dentition full, scissors bite preferred. Level bite acceptable.

Eyes—Almond shaped, set well apart, somewhat slanted. In profile, the eyes are set slightly below the plane of the muzzle. Lids tight, haws should not show. Dark brown, the

darker the better.

Ears—V-shaped, tip is slightly rounded. Rather thick, they are well set back between the level of the eye and the top of the head. When pulled forward the tip of the ear should cover the eye. Looking at the dog face to face, the widest part of the ear is about level to the eye. The inner edge of the ear lies close to the cheek, the outer edge slightly away from the head forming a V. The ears should hold their set and

In general appearance and ability, the Italian Maremma is very similar to its Hungarian cousin, the Kuvasz.

are not cast backward. The ears should not protrude above the head.

NECK—Muscular, without dewlap, medium length, arched at the crest.

FOREQUARTERS— Shoulders muscular. The scapula and humerus form a right angle, are long and of equal length. Legs are medium boned, straight and well muscled. Elbows are neither in nor out. When viewed from the side, the forechest protrudes slightly in front of the shoulders. The joints are dry, hard.

Dewclaws on the forelegs should not be removed.

BODY—Forechest is well developed, chest deep with well-sprung ribs reaching almost to the elbows. Shoulders long with withers higher than back. Back is of medium length, straight, firm and quite broad. The loin is short, muscular and tight. The croup is well muscled, slightly sloping. The brisket is deep, well developed and runs parallel to the ground. The stomach is well tucked up.

BONE—In proportion to the size of the body. Medium, hard. Never heavy or coarse.

HINDQUARTERS—The portion behind the hip joint is moderately long, producing wide, long and strong muscles of the upper thigh. The femur is long, creating well-bent stifles. Lower thigh is long, dry, well muscled. Metatarsus is short, broad and of great strength. Dewclaws, if any, are removed.

TAIL—Carried low, natural length reaching at least to the hocks. In repose, it hangs down resting on the body, the end but slightly lifted. In state of excitement, the tail may be elevated to the level of the loin, the tip slightly curved up. Ideally there should not be much difference in the carriage of the tail in state of excitement or repose.

FEET—Well padded. Pads

It takes imagination to see how such beauty and compla-
cency can turn to fury and brawn. Photo by Isabelle Français. Owner, Nancy L. Eisenberg.

resilient, black. Feet are closed tight forming round "cat feet." The rear paws somewhat longer, some hair between the toes, the less the better. Dark nails are preferred.

SKIN—The skin is heavily pigmented. The more slate gray or black pigmentation the better.

COAT—The Kuvasz has a double coat formed by a guard hair and fine undercoat. The texture of the coat is medium coarse. The coat ranges from quite wavy to straight. Distribution follows a definite pattern of the body regardless of coat type. The head, muzzle, ears and paws are covered with short, smooth hair. The neck has a mane that extends to and covers the chest. Coat on the front of the forelegs up to the elbows and the hind legs below the thighs is short and smooth. The backs of the forelegs are feathered to the

Isn't it easy to place these two white Kuvaszok out on the prairie with the woolly masses?

Sturdy and well-balanced, the Kuvasz is the incarnation of strength and activity; never appearing lanky, cobby nor lethargic. Photo, Panther Photographic International.

pastern with hair 2 to 3 inches long. The body and sides of the thigh are covered with a medium-length coat. The back of the thighs and the entire tail is covered with hair 4 to 6 inches long. It is natural for the Kuvasz to lose most of the long coat during hot weather. Full luxuriant coat comes in seasonably, depending on climate.

Summer coat should not be penalized.

Color—White.

FAULTS

The foregoing description is that of the ideal Kuvasz. Any deviation from the above-described dog must be penalized to the extent of the deviation.

THE MASTIFF

BEST OF
BREED
NORTHWESTERN
CONNECTICUT
DOG CLUB
SEPTEMBER 1978
ASHBEY

Opposite: Many of us never get a sense of what an aggressive protector the Mastiff can be. I've seen aggressively protective Mastiffs in action and I can assure you that it is an experience to remember.

Left: The Mastiff has done well in the show ring. It is as patient and obedient as it is awesome. Ch. Deer Run Wycliff.

The term "mastiff" serves two purposes among dog enthusiasts and dog historians around the world. In a very general sense, a mastiff is any one of a number of very large breeds, some of which survive today and some of which are now extinct. In more specific terms, a mastiff is one of the large breeds which has been established on the British Isles for literally millenia. To some extent, we must view our reference to this particular breed as "the Mastiff" as being somewhat subjective as even today the Mastiff is no more mastiff than are many of the world's other mastiffs. As such we can refer to the Neapolitan Mastiff as being Neapolitan, the French Mastiff as being French, the Spanish Mastiff as being Spanish, the German Mastiff as being German, the Tibetan Mastiff as being Tibetan, etc., because each is a regionally distinct expression of the mastiff type. Likewise, we can refer to the British Mastiff as being uniquely British. By doing this, we not only do justice to the British Mastiff enthusiasts but also eliminate unnecessary confusion.

In any event, it is historically clear that all of our Western mastiff breeds are descended from the early mastiffs of the East, and, among these, all evidence suggests that Assyria was the home of the forerunners of all Western mastiff lines. Stone reliefs dating to more than 4000 years ago depict very large, powerfully built, short-haired dogs of the mastiff-type in Assyria and Babylonia. At about this time, Assyrian political power had expanded and the Assyrian empire had become commercially oriented and wealthy. Trading posts were established hundreds of miles away and extensive trade was being conducted with Asia Minor. Following these trade networks, the distribution of early mastiffs beyond the scope of the Eastern world is very probable.

Upon the Roman invasion of Britain in 55 B.C., Caesar describes the Roman legions as having found British Mastiffs fighting beside their masters with impressive ferocity. Some of these dogs were taken back to Rome and used in the arenas to fight against the native fighting dogs. At this task, the British Mastiffs were found to be superior. An account of their success on the part of the British dogs comes to us in the writing of Gratius Faliscus, who wrote in the year 8 A.D. He writes that the dogs of Epirus—the true Molossian dogs—were pitted against the dogs of Britain, which overpowered them. About 20 years later, Strabo wrote of the British dogs used in hunting and in warfare, saying that the dogs had flabby lips and drooping ears.

In *Master of Game* written between 1406 and 1413, Edward, second Duke of York, devoted separate chapters to the Mastiff and to the now extinct breed known in dog history as the Alaunt. Much of the dog literature of today refers to these two breeds as if they were one and the same, but clearly, at the time of Edward, they were not. Interestingly, Edward mentions that the head of the Alaunt should be "great and short," but he does not mention that these characteristics should typify the Mastiff, which, according to today's standards, they should. He does mention, however, the ability of each of these breeds in wild boar hunting; he also stated in his Mastiff chapter that an especially capable hunting dog was produced when the mastiff was crossed with the Alaunt. As the Alaunt unfortunately faded into the oblivion of extinction shortly after this discussion of the breed by Edward, one might wonder if the extinction of the Alaunt was due to absorption into the mastiff stock of the day in the production of boar-hunting dogs. If so, might the unusually large and short head of the modern English Mastiff be at least partially due to the influence of the Alaunt upon its lines? This could very well be the case, but, if it is, we must still account for the similarly

This is Ch. Deer Run Ivan, owned by Tobin Jackson.

BEST OF
BREED
BUCKS COUNTY
KENNEL CLUB
1983
ASHBEY

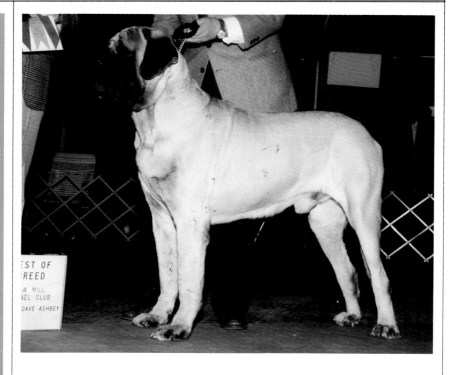

Top: Mastiffs have enjoyed a fine performance record in the conformation ring. Taking Best of Breed is Justin Winston's Ch. Deer Run Ahab. *Bottom:* Ch. Deer Run Police, owned by Zeek Gibbs.

large heads of many other types of Western European mastiffs. Possibly, the already large heads of these dogs were also exaggerated by similar crossing to dogs of the Alaunt type and by crossing to crossbred English Mastiffs.

Considering the Mastiff's long history of combat on the battlefield, in the arena, and in the hunt, it is something of a paradox that the Mastiff of today is as docile as it often is. Certainly there is good reason for many Mastiff owners to prefer to keep more docile dogs, as a 200-pound Mastiff that was allowed to become very aggressive would be uncontrollable in anyone's hands. Yet, it is my feeling that

Taking Best of Winners is Ruth Winston's Ch. Deer Run Durango.

The brindle Mastiff is quite a different looking dog, and is a good alternative to the more common fawn-colored dog. Owner, Elaine Ressa.

a better temperamental balance could have been achieved, and that today's Mastiffs should express more of a protective instinct than they generally do.

One must search carefully in order to find a Mastiff breeder who is concerned with his dog's natural guardian inclination. Once a dog is chosen, an owner must impress upon it, from an early age, the importance of its role as guardian of the home, and yet avoid teaching the animal to become unnecessarily aggressive. Achieving this balance will not be as easy with a Mastiff as it will be with other breeds discussed in this book, so you would do better to avoid this breed if you are in search of a sure-fire, quick-on-the-trigger guard dog.

The Mastiff is not an apartment dog, nor is it a wise choice as a pet for a small house. This is a very large animal, and although it is never very active as an adult, it does need its space. Having said this, let me assure you that I have been to small homes that

contained an entire family, half a dozen full-grown Mastiffs, and a litter of yelping puppies, and everyone was quite content. This is not the way I live, however, and I am much more in favor of bringing home a dog that will fit comfortably in your home rather than a dog that will modify the condition of your home in any way.

The Mastiff is best kept in a large home with at least an acre of property. It is a subdued dog that normally will not stray, but it needs space. It must be well socialized, but its sometimes overly repressed protective nature must be encouraged if it is to become a true guardian. Under these conditions, it is a very fine dog for the house and for the family.

This is a loyal, devoted, and very affectionate breed that is never dangerous to its master and is usually quite safe around older (about eight years old) children. While these dogs are not known to be aggressive toward smaller children, their size alone can overwhelm an adult, and no less a small child.

The size and strength of a Mastiff of good breeding, in good condition, is second to none, and, when the protective nature of one of these dogs is aroused, the Mastiff is certainly an effective man-stopper.

Those in search of a good-looking Mastiff are in a good position, as long as one is willing to invest some time in sorting the good breeding from the poor. While a well-bred Mastiff is a fine dog, a poorly

Tobin Jackson of Deer Run Kennel, a top Mastiff breeder and a true sportsman. With master Tobin is Ch. Deer Run Wycliff.

bred Mastiff will often display a weak, somewhat bovine, overall appearance. As always, the trick is to go to the shows and examine the dogs and their progeny critically.

Standard for the Mastiff

GENERAL APPEARANCE—Large, massive, symmetrical and well-knit frame. A combination of grandeur and good nature, courage and

docility.

HEAD—In general outline giving a massive appearance when viewed from any angle. Breadth to be greatly desired. *Skull*—Broad and somewhat rounded between the ears, forehead slightly curved, showing marked wrinkles which are particularly distinctive when at attention. Brows (superciliary ridges) moderately raised. Muscles of the temples well developed, those of the cheeks extremely powerful. Arch across the skull a flattened curve with a furrow up the center of the forehead. This extends from between the eyes to halfway up the skull. *Ears*—Small, V-shaped, rounded at the tips. Leather moderately thin, set widely apart at the highest points on the sides of the skull continuing the outline across the summit. They should lie close to the cheeks when in repose. Ears dark in color, the blacker the better, conforming to the color of the muzzle.

Eyes—Set wide apart, medium in size, never too prominent. Expression alert but kindly. The stop between the eyes well marked but not too abrupt. Color of eyes brown, the darker the better and showing no haw.

Face and Muzzle—Short, broad under the eyes and running nearly equal in width to the end of the nose. Truncated, *i.e.*, blunt and cut off square, thus forming a right angle with the upper line of the face. Of great depth from the point of the nose to underjaw. Underjaw broad

Ownership of a pair of Mastiffs has as many rewards as it does responsibilities. Are you a fitting candidate for such a role? Photo by Isabelle Français. Owners, John and Donna Bahlman.

The quarters of an animal as large as the Mastiff are of paramount importance to proper movement.

to the end and slightly rounded. Canine teeth healthy, powerful and wide apart. Scissors bite preferred but a moderately undershot jaw permissible providing that the teeth are not visible when the mouth is closed. Lips diverging at obtuse angles with the septum and sufficiently pendulous so as to show a modified square profile. Nose broad and always dark in color, the blacker the better, with spread flat nostrils (not pointed or turned up) in profile. Muzzle dark in color, the blacker the better. Muzzle should be half the length of the skull, thus dividing the head into three parts—one for the foreface and two for the skull. In other words, the distance from tip of nose to stop is equal to one-half the distance between the eyes and nose to that of the head (measured before the ears) as three is to five.

NECK—Powerful and very muscular, slightly arched, and of medium length. The neck gradually increases in circumference as it approaches the shoulder. Neck moderately "dry" (not showing an excess of loose skin).

CHEST AND FLANKS— Wide, deep, rounded and well let down between the forelegs, extending at least to the elbow. Forechest should be deep and well defined.

Ribs extremely well rounded. False ribs deep and well set back. There should be a reasonable, but not exaggerated, cut-up.

SHOULDER AND ARM— Slightly sloping, heavy and muscular. No tendency to looseness of shoulders.

FORELEGS AND FEET— Legs straight, strong and set wide apart, heavy-boned. Elbows parallel to body. Feet heavy, round and compact with well-arched toes. Pasterns strong and bent only slightly. Black nails preferred.

HIND LEGS—Hindquarters broad, wide and muscular. Second thighs well developed, hocks set back, wide apart and parallel when viewed from the rear.

BACK AND LOINS—Back muscular, powerful and straight. Loins wide and muscular, slightly rounded over the rump.

TAIL—Set on moderately high and reaching to the hocks or a little below. Wide at the root, tapering to the end, hanging straight in repose, forming a slight curve but never over the back when dog is in action.

COAT—Outer coat moderately coarse. Undercoat, dense, short and close lying.

Color—Apricot, silver fawn or dark fawn-brindle. Fawn-brindle should have fawn as a background color which should be completely covered with very dark stripes. In any case, muzzle, ears and nose must be dark in color, the blacker the better, with similar color tone around the orbits, extending upwards between them.

SIZE—Dogs, minimum, 30 inches at the shoulder; bitches, minimum, 27½ inches at the shoulder.

GAIT—The gait denotes power and strength. The rear legs should have drive, while the forelegs should track smoothly with good reach. In motion, the legs move straight forward; as the dog's speed increases from a walk to a trot, the feet move in under the center line of the body to maintain balance.

Too much dog for many homes, the Mastiff is best kept in a home with a large yard. Owner, Sandra D. Mansfield.

THE NEAPOLITAN MASTIFF

Everything about the Neapolitan Mastiff, often called the Italian Mastiff, the Italian Bulldog, or simply the Neo, suggests top notch suitability as a guard dog. First and foremost, the Neapolitan is a super-loyal family dog. While

will spend long periods whimpering pitifully until everyone is together again.

The Neapolitan is also an extraordinarily intelligent dog with a great ability to distinguish its friends from its enemies. Don't let the droopy face of the Neapolitan fool you into thinking that the dog is a dullard. Nothing could be further from the truth.

As a deterrent against crime, the Neapolitan Mastiff is as perfect as a dog can be. Its overall appearance, both head and body, suggests a potential for unprecedented brutality and, while the dog is exceptionally gentle around its family and friends, this brutality can easily be realized should the Neapolitan's home or family be seriously threatened. Its size is also a substantial deterrent. A good Neapolitan should stand on short but massive legs, and, though it is relatively low to the ground, a large dog will weigh about 200 pounds. Every inch of the dog suggests terrific power which is put to work even as the dog moves casually.

the breed is generally suspicious of strangers and politely tolerant of friends, it becomes enamored of its human family, particularly of its one master. In fact, among the many Neapolitan Mastiffs I have known, if I have detected any problem at all with the breed's devotion to its family, I would have to say that the problem is that these dogs tend to really miss their owners when they are left alone and

Functionally, the Neapolitan Mastiff is even more capable than its appearance suggests. When you examine a Neapolitan closely, you will realize that, in spite of its heavy appearance and deliberate movement, this is a dog that can really spring into action like a shot should something unexpected happen. Its heavy muscle is very obvious, even though its tough skin is loose and does not connect to the underlying tissue, as does the skin of other dogs. The head of the Neapolitan is huge, the jaws are short and powerful, and the teeth are big and strong. In general, this is most definitely not a dog you want to find yourself face to face with as you step through a stranger's window in order to burglarize his home.

Historically, the Neapolitan Mastiff is among the most interesting of all breeds. Probably descended from the great mastiffs that Alexander the Great regarded so highly in Greece, the early Neapolitan Mastiffs are described in literature of the Roman era as having been used in Rome as gladiator dogs in the arena and in war, as well as in homes as guardians. A description of the Neapolitan in its role as home guardian in Rome comes to us, through the centuries, in the writing of Columella: "The guard dog for the house should be dark in color so that during the day a prowler can see him and be frightened by his appearance. When night falls, the dog, lost in the shadows, can attack without being seen. The head is so massive that it seems to be the most important part of the body. The ears fall toward the front, the brilliant and penetrating eyes are black or gray, the chest is deep and hairy, the hind legs are powerful, the front legs are

Above all things, it is the bond these dogs form with their masters that truly defines the breed. Owner, Zeek Gibbs.

THE NEAPOLITAN MASTIFF

covered with long, thick hair, and he is short-legged with strong toes and nails."

Caesar also describes finding fierce mastiff dogs fighting alongside their masters against the Roman legions during the Roman invasion of Britain in 55 B.C. Many of these British fighting mastiffs were brought back to Rome for use in the arena against the native fighting dogs. At this task, the British

dogs proved to be superior. As such, it is likely that today's Neapolitan Mastiff contains much of the blood of these ancient British dogs as well as the blood of the indigenous Roman breed, for breeders of the ancient Roman fighting dogs would have taken advantage of the best qualities of each breed in the composition of the ultimate arena dog.

Neapolitan Mastiff enthusiasts of modern times owe the preservation of these dogs to a writer by the name of Scanziani, who, recognizing the value of the breed, began breeding the best remaining Neapolitan Mastiff stock in Italy at his kennels in Rome in 1949. A breed standard proposed by Scanziani was accepted by the Italian Kennel Club, but has since been modified.

Excellent Neapolitan Mastiff stock is being bred in Italy today, but the best is often very difficult to obtain if one is an outsider, especially a foreigner, and is very expensive in any event. Fortunately, as quite a few Neapolitan Mastiff enthusiasts have close ties to Italy, some of Italy's best bloodlines are available. A well-bred dog is still fairly expensive, but really no more than any well-bred show dog.

However, the Neapolitan Mastiff is not a breed for everyone. I feel it necessary to warn prospective Neapolitan Mastiff owners that these dogs salivate more than any other breed that I am aware of and often tend to be incredibly messy eaters. In view of their extraordinary size, these characteristics render the Neapolitan absolutely unsuitable as an indoor dog unless it is to have an area of a large home that is primarily its own. These dogs are most at home on an estate or in any home surrounded by a large piece of property. In such an environment, they are among the world's greatest man-stopping guard dogs.

Standard for the Neapolitan Mastiff

GENERAL APPEARANCE—The Neapolitan Mastiff must give the impression of great strength and symmetry. It is of very reliable temperament unless provoked, yet sustains all the fine qualities any dog needs for a family companion. He should be bold, discerning, and capable of performing working dog duties.

HEAD—Massive with a broad, flat, short skull. The length of the muzzle should be no more than one-third the length of the head. The directions of the upper

longitudinal axis of the skull and muzzle are parallel. The skull is abundant with wrinkles and folds. The nose should be generous with large and well-opened nostrils. The pigmentation of the nose varies with the color of the coat. Black in black-coated dogs, dark in others. Brown in all dogs having a mahogany coat. The lips are thick textured, full, and heavy. The upper lips, seen from the front, are shaped like an inverted "V." The jaws are strong, well developed, and meeting in either a scissor bite or an even bite. The underjaw is powerful.

Eyes—The color of the eyes is hazel but may correspond to the color of

A family's best friend and an intruder's worst nightmare is an accurate way to describe the Neapolitan Mastiff.

Top: Tobin Jackson with a phenomenally typy Neapolitan. *Bottom:* Maurice Jones trains these monsters for guard work. I know both of these men well and they both sure know these dogs.

the dog's coat. The expression of the Neapolitan Mastiff when alert should be penetrating and hard. The eyelids should be normally close fitting. The eyes, set in a subfrontal position, are well separated from each other and are rather rounded, in spite of the oval appearance given by the abundant skin surrounding them. They are fairly deep set. The pigmentation of the eyelids is black, blue, or brown, depending on the color of the coat.

Ears—Small in comparison to the size of the dog. Triangular, set on well above the zygomatic arch. If not clipped, they hang flat adhering to the cheeks and the partoid region. In length, they should not extend beyond the edge of the throat. The ear rises abruptly at the insertion point and then falls with equal suddenness. In clipping the ear, it is almost amputated to the point where it forms a nearly equilateral triangle.

NECK—The neck should be short, stocky, and extraordinarily muscular. The lower side of the neck

When a Neapolitan Mastiff is put together right, it is an absolutely awesome animal to behold. Owner, Dr. Querci.

has much loose skin, which forms a dewlap, which should be neither too abundant nor undivided. The dewlap begins at the lower jaw and reaches approximately the midpoint of the neck.

BODY—Chest, broad and well developed. Ribs, well sprung and broad, descending to the level of the elbow and slightly below. The last back ribs are long, sloping, and well open. The top line is straight and only the withers rise above it. Loins well let into the back line, slightly rounded as seen in profile, with well developed muscling in their width. The line of the belly is nearly horizontal. In profile, the dog should be rectangular rather than square.

FOREQUARTERS—The shoulders should be long, and slightly sloped with long muscles, well developed, and well separated from each other and free in their movements. Its slope is 50–60° from the horizontal. In respect to the medial plane of the body, the points of the scapulae are fairly separated from each other, tending rather to be vertical to that plane. The elbows should be straight, vertical, and exceptionally well muscled, and flat against the body. Front legs, straight with massive bone. Feet, compact, large, and oval shaped, with thick pads. Pasterns slightly bent.

HINDQUARTERS—Broad, well developed. Thigh, long, well muscled, and powerful. Stifles well bent. Hocks, well let down and parallel to each other when viewed from behind.

GAIT—The movement is one of the characteristics of the breed. It is slow, free, and bear-like. The trot is slow with long steps, covering a good deal of ground. Viewed from both front and back, legs should move parallel to each other.

TAIL—The tail is thick at the root, robust, and slightly tapered toward the tip. In repose, the tail should be carried as a saber tail, that is, hanging slightly curved in the lower third. It is never carried over the back, but horizontal or very slightly above the backline when the dog is in action. Its length is equal to or slightly more than the distance to the hock. It is docked to about two-thirds of its length.

COAT—The hair should be dense, equal in length, smooth throughout, fine or flat. There should be no sign of fringe in any part of the body, legs, or tail. The texture is harsh.

Color—Permissible colors are black, blue, gray, mahogany, and brindle, with white spots allowed on the chest and on the tips of the toes. The pigmentation of the nose and eyelid should be blue or brown, depending on the darkest markings on the coat.

FAULTS

Any departure from the aforementioned points shall be considered a fault and the seriousness of the fault shall be in exact proportion to its degree.

DISQUALIFICATIONS

Height at the shoulders, more than 30 inches or less than 23 inches. Total discoloration of the nose. Nasal bridge decidedly arched or hollowed. Wall eye. Discoloration of the eyelids. Cross-eyes. Lack of dewlap. Extensive white coat or white on the face.

Always on the alert despite their droopy appearance. This is an extremely intelligent breed. Photo by Isabelle Français.

THE ROTTWEILER

Opposite: **The Rottweiler is an old breed that began in Germany as a cattle drover. Today it rivals the best of dogs as a companion and guardian. Owner, "Luger" Schwartz.**

Left: **To see a large, athletic Rottweiler move is to put many of the large breeds to shame. These dogs weigh the same as a Bullmastiff— have you ever seen a Bullmastiff jump like this?!**

The region of Württemberg in western Germany produces two living things of which I am particularly fond. One is a wonderful red wine made from the Trollinger grape (yes, wine is a living thing); the other is an excellent man-stopping guard dog that will also be a joy to have lying at your side while you are sipping your glass of Trollinger—it is the Rottweiler, one of the finest man-stopping guard dogs ever developed anywhere.

Named after the town of Rottweil, which is thought to be roughly the modern center of distribution of the breed, the Rottweiler is of ancient origin and its exact composition is lost to time. We do know, however, that this area of Germany was an important military center for the Romans, and it is believed that the most basic component breed used in the production of today's Rottweiler dog was the mastiff-type dogs used for herding and defense by the Romans and brought north by the Roman military. Local component breeds may or may not have been added to this original bloodline, but it is uncertain which breeds, if any, were added.

It is likely that the ancestors of today's Rottweiler dog served the primary function of driving cattle until relatively recent times. During the

The Rottweiler, whose ancestors functioned as droving dogs in Germany until relatively recent years, is growing in popularity in the United States perhaps faster than any other breed of dog.

middle of the nineteenth century, the driving of cattle was made illegal and the donkey began to take the place of the dog as the beast of burden used to pull carts. As a result, the Rottweiler population began to decline rapidly until it appeared to reach a condition of near extinction shortly before the beginning of the twentieth century. Fortunately, this situation changed even more quickly than it developed. The first decade of the twentieth century saw a sharp increase in the use of the Rottweiler as a police dog. By 1921, there were 3400 Rottweilers registered by a few separate German Rottweiler dog clubs. It appears that many of the dogs listed in the roster of one of these clubs were also registered by the other clubs, but the formation of the Allgemeiner Deutscher Rottweiler Klub and the production of its stud book in 1924 rectified this situation.

Although the Rottweiler population was again severely decimated during World War II, the breed did survive, and some credit must go to foreign breeders and enthusiasts for this. The American Kennel Club admitted the first Rottweiler to its stud book in 1931, and the breed standard was adopted in 1935. The breed has increased steadily in popularity since that time, and recently there has been a veritable explosion in its popularity. Considering the fact that the Rottweiler is such a large breed, this great growth in popularity speaks very highly for the many positive qualities of the Rottweiler. As we have seen with other popular breeds, and as we observe in the case of the Rottweiler, the great

When you see a Rottie muzzled, you can figure that the owner may well not be kidding. The Rottie is not only large, agile and powerful, but it is known to have a hard bite. These well-trained Rotties are participating in the 1986 World Dog Show.

THE ROTTWEILER

popularity of a purebred—particularly instant popularity—is too often a negative development. As the demand for a breed increases, breeders who are less sincere about producing fine dogs are attracted to the breed by the chance to cash in on puppy production. For such breeders, profits can be increased if the cost of breeding stock can be reduced, and the easiest method of reducing these costs is to settle for lower quality stock. Puppies produced are, of course, also of lesser quality,

and the overall quality of the breed steadily diminishes. Especially in the case of a traditionally expensive breed like the Rottweiler, prospective buyers are too often attracted by the opportunity to obtain a puppy from a less reputable breeder for less money. If you are unwilling to pay the high prices often asked for Rotty pups, select another of the great guardian breeds, but never compromise on the quality of any pup of any breed!

While this may all have sounded somewhat

discouraging, I feel it is necessary to discuss, as this breed in particular is experiencing such a general transition in quality. But suppose you do find a well-bred Rottweiler. What have you got then?

A well-bred Rottweiler not only is a truly magnificent show dog but also is among the finest of all man-stopping guard dogs. It is a large but compact, short-haired breed that is easy to own as an indoor dog and suitable for yard life (given adequate shelter) as well. It is a fast-moving, powerful breed with a tremendously powerful bite (roughly twice as powerful as that of a German Shepherd or a Doberman Pinscher), and it is the perfect combination of steady temperament and willingness to defend. This is a breed that is quick-on-the-trigger when a situation that calls for instant defense arises and yet it is a good, laid-back family dog on a 24-hour basis. It is an intelligent breed with a definite preference for its immediate family, and it is a guard dog of the greatest

Officer Mike Howard works his Angus vom Hochfeld (known also as "Grizzly"). This accomplished Rottie worked as a police dog for the El Cajon Police Department. Photo courtesy of Grizzly's breeder Vivian Peters.

THE ROTTWEILER

ability. If it is a sure-fire guard dog you are in the market for, be sure to include the Rottweiler at the top of your shopping list.

Standard for the Rottweiler

GENERAL APPEARANCE—The ideal Rottweiler is a large, robust and powerful dog, black with clearly defined rust markings. His compact build denotes great strength, agility and endurance. Males are characteristically larger, heavier boned and more masculine in appearance.

SIZE—Males—24 to 27 inches. Females—22 to 25 inches. Proportion should always be considered rather than height alone. The length of the body from the breastbone (sternum) to the rear edge of the pelvis (ischium) is slightly longer than the height of the dog at the withers; the most desirable proportion being 10 to 9. Depth of chest should be fifty percent of the height. **Serious Faults**—Lack of proportion, undersize, oversize.

HEAD—Of medium length, broad between the ears;

In the show ring, the Rottweiler must have all 42 teeth. Strong jaws meeting in a definitive scissors bite accommodate the dog's protection work too. These dogs bite hard.

forehead line seen in profile is moderately arched. Cheekbones and stop well developed; length of muzzle should not exceed distance between stop and occiput. Skull is preferred dry; however, some wrinkling may occur when dog is alert.

Muzzle—Bridge is straight, broad at base with slight tapering towards tip. Nose is broad rather than round, with black nostrils.

Lips—Always black; corners tightly closed. Inner mouth pigment is dark. A pink mouth is to be penalized.

Teeth—42 in number (20 upper and 22 lower); strong, correctly placed, meeting in a scissors bite— lower incisors touching inside of upper incisors. **Serious Faults**—any

missing tooth, level bite. **Disqualifications**— undershot, overshot, four or more missing teeth.

Eyes—Of medium size, moderately deep set, almond shaped with well-fitting lids. Iris of uniform

In addition to being able, intelligent and trainable, the Rottweiler is handsome and affectionate.

color, from medium to dark brown, the darker shade always preferred.

Serious Faults—Yellow (bird of prey) eyes; eyes unequal in size or shape. Hairless lid.

Ears—Pendant, proportionately small, triangular in shape; set well apart and placed on skull so as to make it appear broader when the dog is alert. Ear terminated at approximately mid-cheek level. Correctly held, the inner edge will lie tightly against cheek.

NECK—Powerful, well muscled, moderately long with slight arch and without loose skin.

BODY—Topline is firm and level, extending in straight line from withers to croup.

Brisket—Deep, reaching to elbow.

Chest—Roomy, broad with well-pronounced forechest.

Ribs—Well sprung.

Loin—Short, deep, well muscled.

Croup—Broad, medium length, slightly sloping.

TAIL—Normally carried in horizontal position—giving impression of an elongation of top line. Carried slightly above horizontal when dog is excited. Some dogs are born without a tail, or a very short stub. Tail is normally docked short, close to the body. The set of the tail is more important than the length.

FOREQUARTERS—Shoulder blade—long, well laid back at 45 degree angle. Elbows tight, well under body. Distance from withers to elbow and elbow to ground is equal.

Legs—Strongly developed with straight heavy bone. Not set closely together.

Pasterns—Strong, springy and almost perpendicular to the ground.

Feet—Round, compact, well

A well-bred Rottweiler can move like the wind. This is Am. and Can. Ch. Ivan von Gruenerwald. Owner, Forrest Wells.

arched toes, turning neither in nor out. Pads thick and hard; nails short, strong and black. Dewclaws may be removed.

HINDQUARTERS— Angulation of hindquarters matches that of forequarters. *Upper Thigh*—Fairly long, broad and well muscled. *Stifle Joint*—Moderately angulated. *Lower Thigh*—Long, powerful, extensively muscled leading into a strong hock joint; metatarsus nearly perpendicular to the ground. Viewed from rear, hind legs are straight and wide enough apart to fit in with a properly built body. *Feet*—Somewhat longer than front feet, well arched toes turning neither in nor out. Dewclaws must be removed if present.

COAT—Outer coat is straight, coarse, dense, medium

A well-bred Rottie is a great choice as a breed that combines unparalleled guardian ability with stability and close binding. Am. and Can. Ch. Quick von Siegerhaus owned by Thom and Carol Woodward.

length, lying flat. Undercoat must be present on neck and thighs, but should not show through the outer coat. The Rottweiler should be exhibited in a natural condition without trimming, except to remove whiskers, if desired. **Fault**—Wavy coat **Serious Faults**—Excessively short coat, curly or open coat; lack of under coat. **Disqualification**—Long coat. *Color*—Always black with rust to mahogany markings. The borderline between black and rust should always be clearly defined. The markings should be located as follows: a spot over each eye; on cheeks, as a strip around each side of the muzzle, but not on the bridge of the nose; on throat; triangular mark on either side of breastbone; on forelegs from carpus downward to toes; on

The Rottweiler's chest should be broad with a well-pronounced forechest. Photo by Isabelle Français. Dog handled by Stephen Wojculewski.

inside of rear legs showing down the front of stifle and broadening out to front of rear legs from hock to toes; but not completely eliminating black from back of legs; under tail. Black penciling markings on toes. The undercoat is gray or black.

Quantity and location of rust markings is important and should not exceed ten percent of body color.

Insufficient or excessive markings should be penalized. **Serious Faults—** Excessive markings; white markings any place on dog (a few white hairs do not constitute a marking); light colored markings.

Disqualification—Any base color other than black; total absence of markings.

GAIT—The Rottweiler is a trotter. The motion is harmonious, sure, powerful

The popularity of the Rottweiler as a guard dog extends international boundaries; good looks and trainability cannot be denied. Am., Bda. Ch. Von Gailingen's Dark Delight, U.D.T., Bda. C.D.X. and Can. C.D., is owned by Carol M. Thompson.

DOG TRAINING CLUB OF BERMUDA

and unhindered, with a strong forereach and a powerful rear drive. Front and rear legs are thrown neither in nor out, as the imprint of hind feet should touch that of forefeet. In a trot, the forequarters and hindquarters are mutually coordinated while the back remains firm; as speed is increased legs will converge under body towards a center line.

CHARACTER—The Rottweiler should possess a fearless expression with a self assured aloofness that does not lend itself to immediate and indiscriminate friendships. He has an inherent desire to protect home and family, and is an intelligent dog of extreme

hard ness and adaptability with a strong willingness to work.

A judge shall dismiss from the ring any shy or vicious Rottweiler.

Shyness—A dog shall be judged fundamentally shy if, refusing to stand for examination, it shrinks away from the judge; if it fears an approach from the rear; if it shies at sudden or unusual noises to a marked degree.

Viciousness—A dog that attacks or attempts to attack either the judge or its handler is definitely vicious. An aggressive or belligerent attitude towards other dogs shall not be deemed viciousness.

THE SPANISH MASTIFF

Opposite: Dr. Sewerin of Germany working a good Spanish Mastiff.

Left: The appearance of a good Spanish Mastiff is awesome. Wouldn't you think that Americans would want to know more about these dogs? Photo by Carlos Salas Melero.

The Spanish Mastiff is another expression of the ancient mastiff dogs that have existed throughout Europe for millenia. It is a breed which many purebred enthusiasts generally know very little about, other than the bits of information that can sometimes be found in the rare breed sections of some dog encyclopedias. This is primarily due to the fact that the breed in its pure form is extremely rare

THE SPANISH MASTIFF

A Spanish Mastiff in its natural environment, doing what it was developed to do. Spanish shepherds developed these dogs for flock protection purposes and virtually would never give a puppy to a non-shepherd. Photo courtesy of R. Coppinger.

and that, until recently, the only way to get one was to be a Spanish shepherd who needed one. It was then likely that another Spanish shepherd who recognized your need would give you one, but even then it was unlikely to be purebred.

It has only been for the past few years that Spanish purebred enthusiasts have paid much attention to the maintenance of this breed. These enthusiasts claim that there are currently as many as 15,000 Mastines Españoles in Spain, but reliable estimates put the number of mixed breed dogs among these 15,000 as being as high as 98%. As many of the large herding breeds and

the Saint Bernard are often crossed into the Spanish Mastiff lines, purchasing a purebred representative of one of these dogs is a very risky business. Even a casual visit to Spain and a deal worked out with a shepherd will often lead one astray. It is not that Spanish shepherds intentionally mislead prospective buyers of Mastín puppies so much as the difference between what a shepherd means when he refers to a Spanish Mastiff and what a purebred enthusiast means when he refers to the same dog. If it is your objective to purchase your own Spanish Mastiff in Spain from a Spanish shepherd, you had better be

very fond of walking, climbing (as the best Mastín are found in the northern mountains around Léon), sheep, and fleas. You must also be very fluent in Spanish, an excellent bargainer, and prepared to spend at least six weeks in Spain searching for a good dog. Of course, you should know what a good dog is before you go.

Fortunately, all of this is not necessary, as show and guard dog breeders have become involved in keeping the Mastín, but, again, one should choose only the most reputable dealers in order to secure purebred stock. Limited breeding stock is available in the United States. Some good Mastín are available in Spain, but, much to the dismay of many Spanish breeders, the very best purebred Mastín stock is currently available in Germany. Furthermore, it is likely that the breed will remain intact in Germany for a long time to come.

The Mastín Español is one of the largest breeds in the world today. I realize the exaggerated size statistics we are often quoted by show Mastiff breeders who will tell you their dog is 265 pounds, as you stand right before the dog that you can plainly see is no bigger than 200 pounds; I also realize that

THE SPANISH MASTIFF

These are obviously not a good selection for everyone in search of a guard dog, but if you've got the room and the inclination, it should certainly be a consideration. Photo by Carlos Salas Melero.

dog encyclopedias have been known to offer a size of 200 pounds for Tibetan Mastiffs, while a figure of half that size would be more appropriate. Nevertheless, my very reliable, first-hand sources in Europe, who have surveyed the northern mountains of Spain as well as the show rings for the best Mastín, tell me that a large male Mastín Español can easily reach 90 centimeters (nearly three feet) at the withers and weigh 100 kg. (220 pounds). Minimum heights for males should be 77 centimeters (30½ inches) and for females 73 centimeters (almost 29 inches). A male should weigh no less than about 176 pounds and a female no less than about 154

pounds. One of these animals is a great deal of dog to have around the house, yet the breed is ideally suited for a house in a suburban area with a large backyard where the dog can pass most of its time undisturbed. The breed is very resistant to extremes in temperature and is very comfortable outdoors, but it can also be kept indoors in order to guard the house (with no problem) while the family is away. As with any breed, the Mastín must be socialized as an indoor dog in order to respond well to indoor life. These dogs do not need a great deal of exercise in order to stay in shape, but a daily walking of at least three miles is necessary for the maintenance of any large breed.

As a family dog, the Mastín Español is excellent. It is generally a people-loving dog that enjoys the company of its human family. It is not a dog to stray when given the opportunity to do so, but, rather, it prefers to walk by its master's side. It is known as a breed that is gentle with children and with family pets, including cats, but the sight of a strange dog will often drive the Mastín wild, and it will fight fierce battles with any strange dog that trespasses upon its territory. We must remember that the primary duty of this dog is to protect a flock against predatory wolves, so attacking strange dogs is instinctive to the Mastín. A good Spanish Mastiff can easily catch and kill a wolf singlehandedly. As a result, it would be very wise to keep your Mastín away from your neighbor's German Shepherd unless you enjoy spending time in court.

As a guard dog, the Mastín is absolutely excellent. The breed is suspicious of strangers, devoted to its home and family,

The Spanish Mastiff is powerful and protective. Photo by Carlos Salas Melero.

and utterly fearless. It is a quiet dog that reserves its barking for the real thing, and it is a calm, steady dog as well.

This is clearly a breed that is suitable to occupy the attention currently enjoyed by such breeds as the Saint Bernard, the Newfoundland, and other very

prove a source of pride and pleasure.

Standard for the Spanish Mastiff

GENERAL CHARACTERISTICS—

A beautiful Spanish Mastiff.

large breeds known to purebred enthusiasts. Once again, I would strongly advise anyone who is inclined to own one of these beautiful animals to be careful making your selection, but not be deterred by the difficulty of finding useful stock. Although quality may be difficult to find, the Mastín will

In appearance the Spanish Mastiff should be robust, stocky, symmetrical, and in no sense obese. The gait should give impression of power and agility.

SIZE—Weight: 110–132 lbs. Height: 25½–27½ inches. Females are generally shorter and lighter than males.

HEAD—Well built and in good proportion. The skull is broad, slightly rounded, long with a rather long muzzle; the nose is black. The lips are full, especially the lower lips, which form two pendulous pouches at the commissure; these pouches are rounded, wet, very black with pink at the edges. The jaws are powerful; the molars are large and sound. The other teeth should be small and white, except for the canine, which are large and well set for taking prey. The stop is not pronounced but should be well defined.

Eyes—Small and intelligent; the lachrimal pouch is loosely attached and falls in a pronounced manner, showing a great deal of haw.

Ears—Small, stout at the base, hanging; they are pointed at the tips.

NECK—Strong, muscular and flexible, with abundant loose skin, which forms two large pouches at the throat; these pouches are identical and well divided by a deep furrow; they are soft to the touch.

FOREQUARTERS—Strong, muscular, well-formed shoulders. The legs are well shaped, strong, but not coarse, with the muscles and tendons very much in evidence. The forearms are straight and moderately long, stout at the joint and less so at the extremities. The forefeet are not very large or long; the toes and knuckles are well defined.

TAIL—Strong and flexible, with long, thick hair forming a flag; it is moderately thick and carried low, with a slight curve at the end when the dog is in repose. It is carried high and proudly when the dog is animated, but it should never curl over the back.

HINDQUARTERS—Long and well positioned, forming almost a right angle with the body; strong and well muscled in the upper part, fine and well shaped in the lower. Vertical and parallel, with no tendency to cowhocks.

A broad and slightly rounded skull with a powerful jaw is described in the breed standard. Photo by Carlos Salas Melero.

THE SPANISH MASTIFF

The brindle coat, known in Spanish as "tigre" (or tiger) is especially interesting when occurring on this breed. I've always been partial to brindle dogs. Photo by Carlos Salas Melero.

FEET—Without dewclaws; they set well on the ground and are short, with well-shaped toes.

COAT—Not long, but fine and thick, soft to the touch, with a short fringe behind and on the back part of the forelegs.

Color—Varies widely with this breed. The commoner colors being reddish, wolf gray, fawn, white and black, white and golden yellow, white and gray, grizzle. In dark coats, the hair should be of a lighter shade at the roots.

SKIN—Rosy white.

FAULTS—Nose mottled or not black; muzzle too pointed; badly adapted. Jaws ill-equipped for seizing; excessive saddleback; short tail or tail carried over the back; weak or crooked legs; cowhocks; excessively long or woolly hair.

"TIGRE"
FOTO: CARLOS SALAS
1983

Top: Abundantly adorned with loose skin, the dog's neck is both muscular and flexible. Photo by Carlos Salas Melero. *Bottom:* A massive and elegant Spanish Mastiff. Photo by Isabelle Français. Owner, Pedro Perez Soriano.

THE TIBETAN MASTIFF

Opposite: Perhaps the most ancient of all guardians, the Tibetan Mastiff comes to the service of our twentieth-century homes from the Tibet of centuries ago. Photo by Isabelle Français. Owners, Donald and Louise Skilton.

Left: To see a large well-bred Tibetan Mastiff like this one move is to learn a lesson about what a big dog can be.

The Tibetan Mastiff is the most generally misunderstood breed that we will be discussing and is undoubtedly one of the most generally misunderstood breeds in existence today. Its history is among the most ancient of all breeds, and its contribution to the development of so many other modern breeds is second

Strong, beautiful, and as free-moving as the wind is the Tibetan Mastiff. Owner, Gichhorn Maynard.

book depiction. One should also keep one's eye fixed on the future when viewing much of today's Tibetan Mastiff stock.

The most striking difference between the textbook depiction of a Tibetan and the actual Tibetan of today is size. As I am writing this chapter, I have, open before me, the Tibetan Mastiff section of one current, very popular all-breed book. It says of the size of the Tibetan that the breed may reach nearly 220 pounds. Someone, I dare say, has not seen many Tibetan Mastiffs. But such gross exaggerations of weight are typical of dog people, especially of mastiff breed enthusiasts, and in the case of the Tibetan, exaggeration has become the norm.

In actuality, among modern show stock, a large male Tibetan Mastiff will not weigh more than 100 pounds. One exceptional black and tan male whelped in England during the 1930s (called "Bru") stood 30 inches at the withers and weighed 140 pounds or so. This male is often hailed as having represented the perfect Tibetan Mastiff type and size.

Recently, a couple of close personal friends of mine went off on a wonderful vacation to Katmandu, Nepal. Fortunately, these friends were great dog (especially rare-breed) enthusiasts, and before they left we discussed the value of keeping a sharp eye out for unusual dogs, especially dogs of the Tibetan Mastiff type. Off they went, and I anxiously

to none. It is high time that today's breeders put forth a serious effort to establish this breed as a fully accepted and clearly understood purebred; but first we must decide precisely what these dogs should be.

The first thing that the armchair Tibetan Mastiff enthusiast will learn upon viewing a Tibetan is that these dogs don't look at all like what most of us will expect based on our reading. As such, one's first look at a Tibetan can be a very disappointing experience (I know mine was) unless one is prepared to see something quite different than the average dog-

awaited information on Tibetans in their native land. I did not expect the kind of information they relayed to me upon their return.

Apparently, in Katmandu and the surrounding area, the Tibetan Mastiff type dog is extremely common. The unusual thing is that large dogs are quite rare. While my friends tracked down one Tibetan male that, with its long coat of matted hair, offered the appearance of being nearly as large as a St. Bernard, most were much smaller. In fact, the majority of these dogs weighed as little as *30 pounds* or slightly more!

The fact that today's Tibetan Mastiffs are not really very tall dogs (normally about 25 to 27 inches at the withers for a good male, about the size of a German Shepherd), not especially heavy bodied dogs as compared to other modern mastiffs, and not nearly as stout in the muzzle as other of today's mastiffs has led many purebred fanciers to wonder about the validity of referring to these dogs as mastiffs at all.

A good Tibetan winning a show. I wasn't there but I bet he deserved it. Photo by Marilyn Harned.

One expression of this doubt was offered by David Hancock of the *English Kennel Gazette*, who proposed that the name of the breed should be officially changed to "Tibetan Mountain Dog."

Mr. Hancock may well have a point worthy of serious consideration. In my opinion, the resolution to this question lies in the reconstructable history of the breed. If we can find evidence that both extremely large dogs and much smaller dogs, each of the "Tibetan" type, did exist prior to the collection of these dogs for show and other aesthetic purposes, then we may well be dealing with two very valid purebreds i.e., the "Tibetan Mastiff" and the "Tibetan Mountain Dog," if you will. It

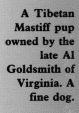

A Tibetan Mastiff pup owned by the late Al Goldsmith of Virginia. A fine dog.

appears to me that this may very well be the case.

The first question we must answer in our consideration of the "Tibetan Dog" hypothesis is: where did the belief that huge Tibetan dogs once existed arise? We know for a fact through modern observation that the smaller variety is well represented throughout the Himalayan region. It seems that it was Marco Polo, in his travels east during the thirteenth century, who first described the huge dogs of Tibet in western literature. Marco Polo says of these dogs that they were as big as donkeys. This piece of writing has been quoted innumerable times by dog historians as being evidence that mastiff dogs existed in Tibet prior to modern times. I wonder how many of us have actually read Marco Polo? While I do believe that the man did come across roughly mastiff-sized dogs in Tibet, the proportions of these dogs that he offers should hardly be taken as gospel truth. In fact, while it is common knowledge that Marco Polo's writing is based on solid experience, my impression of his travelogue is that it is best viewed as being largely intended to impress the folks back home with the wonders of the Orient while remaining as factual as possible.

One interesting bit of information which sheds light on the question of Tibetan Mastiff size appeared in a German publication not very long ago. Apparently, the

stuffed and mounted head of a Tibetan Mastiff was discovered hanging on the wall of the "Dog and Muffler Pub" near Monmouth, England, close to the Welsh border. This dog had been brought, alive, to England from India in 1908.

A stunning black and tan Tibetan Mastiff. Notice the length of coat on the head.

Measurements of the head were taken and are as follows:

Distance from stop to end of muzzle: 4 inches

Girth of skull: 28½ inches

Girth of muzzle: 17 inches

Distance from stop to end of nose: 11½ inches

Distance from ear to ear: 7 inches.
These dimensions describe a big dog.

The description by Marco Polo, the stuffed and mounted head in the "Dog and Muffler Pub," the example of "Bru," and the fact that large Tibetan dogs do exist in the Himalayan region today (although not with thoroughly convincing frequency) all suggest that, in addition to the smaller variety, the mastiff-sized Tibetan dog does have its place in history and so in the modern show ring.

We do know that a population of large dogs did once exist in central Tibet. In the Tibetan language, these dogs were referred to as *Sang-Khyi*. Tibetan dogs that are tied up and used as guard dogs are known as *Do-Khyi*, while those used as shepherds' dogs are known as *Drog-Khyi*.

The Do-Khyi clearly has its place in recent Tibetan history. These dogs were used to protect entire villages of people, particularly women and children while the men of the village were away tending their crops. The dogs are generally very useful as guardians and are esteemed throughout much of the world today; however, they are an independent breed, reserved by nature, and some will feel that they are too aloof to compare to some of the more traditional guard dog breeds as dependable protection.

My own experience with these dogs has been such that I am convinced it is typical of the breed to be highly suspicious of strangers and to sound the alarm upon the sight of a stranger. While these dogs are not overly aggressive, they strike me as being a thinking dog that remains suspicious of strangers for a long time and one that relies upon a very primitive instinct to determine friend from foe.

The word "primitive," in fact, is a very useful one in a description of the Tibetan Mastiff breed. Everything about this dog, other than the fact that it does develop a bond to its human family, suggests a much more primitive nature, overall, than is common among other breeds. The howling bark of these dogs when aroused by the presence of a stranger, their stance when in the presence of a stranger, and their general appearance suggest that half of the mind of the dog in question is thinking in the present while the other half remains in the Himalayas of a century ago and more.

Certainly, a good Tibetan dog of sufficient size could easily develop into a capable man-stopping guardian in a modern Western environment. One must be prepared for the somewhat independent attitude of these dogs in order to avoid disappointment. One must also be prepared to do a great deal of brushing, as this is a very long-coated breed.

I would recommend these dogs for a suburban or rural environment in which a private

"While these dogs are not overly aggressive, they strike me as being a thinking dog that remains suspicious of strangers for a long time and one that relies upon a very primitive instinct of friend and foe."

home with a fenced yard can be provided. Get to know the breed before selection.

Curiously, none of our current American or European Tibetan Mastiff lines can be traced directly to Tibet. All come from the southern side of the Himalayas, from India, Nepal and Bhutan. The breed is registered with the Fédération Cynologique Internationale (F.C.I.), and the first F.C.I. Tibetan Mastiff breed standard was written in the English language.

As more show-oriented Tibetan Mastiff enthusiasts begin to acquire and produce more dogs, it is highly likely that the appearance of the breed will become more like what most presently expect. I would advise anyone interested in these dogs to investigate stock already available, as there are good dogs among this stock.

Standard of the Tibetan Mastiff

GENERAL APPEARANCE—The Tibetan Mastiff is a large, powerful, well-balanced dog. Sturdily built with heavy bone. A breed evolved under the most rigorous of conditions, it should show the structure capable of being able to function on the most difficult of conditions with stamina, speed and agility. Has an alert and noble expression, somewhat reserved.

HEAD—One of the most important features of the Tibetan Mastiff.

Skull—Broad, slightly arched; definite, not steep, stop; well-developed occiput. Supraorbital brow

If I had a few acres of property, I'd like to own a Tibetan. They do shed, mind you. Photo by Isabelle Français. Owners, Donald and Louise Skilton.

well defined in mature dogs. Parietal bones, commonly known as sagital crest, should noticeably diverge from center of skull giving the head an unusual lateral rise that can be felt on the uppermost part of the forehead. Muzzle should be blunt, well cushioned in appearance, shorter than the skull and very powerful.

Nose—Wide, well-developed nostrils (*see* Pigmentation section for color of nose, lips, and eye rims.)

Ears—Pendent, V-shaped though rounded at the tips. Side placement with forward carriage when at attention.

BODY—Heavy in appearance, well balanced.

CHEST—Broad and deep, ribs well sprung but must allow for good movement of shoulders.

NECK—Arched, powerful with moderate dewlap on mature dogs.

SHOULDERS—Moderate angulation.

BACK—Straight and strong; muscular loins slope slightly up to pronounced hips, which are broad. Croup slopes away from spine, but never so steep as to restrict movement on hind legs.

TAIL—Moderately long, reaching to hock. It is profusely feathered with thick long hair and carried forward or to the side in a plume over the back.

FORELEGS—Firm front, heavy bone, straight and well muscled when viewed from side to front. Pasterns slightly bent. Length of leg from ground to elbow about 50% of total height at withers.

HINDQUARTERS—Powerful and well muscled with good length between hips and hocks. Upper thighs well developed and slightly bowed from crotch to hock. Hocks well let down. Viewed from rear, legs are parallel from the hocks down. Stifles show moderate angulation when standing, showing maximum angulation when gaiting.

MOVEMENT—In large deeply bodied dogs the movement appears slow and deliberate at the trot. At the walk, which is distinct and unique in this breed, the Tibetan Mastiff could be considered to have a stalking, determined gait. In motion the legs move straight forward, and, as the dog's speed increases from a walk to a trot, the feet move in under the centerline of the body to maintain balance (single track).

SIZE—*Minimum* height for males is 25 inches; *Minimum* height for bitches is 24 inches; *however*, while large size is preferred, it *should not* take precedence over proper type, balance, soundness and temperament.

COAT—Outer coat should be

harsh, medium length and not shaggy. It is weather-resistant and almost non-shedding. Undercoat is woolly, very thick and when fully developed, so dense that it is almost impossible to see the skin. Coat is climate-related. Dogs in cold climates show heavier undercoat. A longer, heavy-textured, thick and dense coat forms a ruff around the neck, extending to the occiput and mantle down the back from the shoulders to the tail. Front legs may be feathered. Hind legs, from the hock to heel may have somewhat long and thick fur. NOTE: Since this is a natural breed, there is no need for trimming, docking, cropping or shaving. Vibrissae to be left intact for the show ring.

Color—All colors and variations accepted.

PIGMENTATION—Black, black/tan, gold, grizzle and sable dogs must have black lips, nose and eye rims; brown dogs may have liver lips, nose and eye rims. A dudley nose is a major fault; flesh- or pink-colored nose, lips and eye rims are disqualifications.

TEMPERAMENT—The judge shall dismiss from the ring any shy or vicious Tibetan Mastiff

ATMA Membership-Approved—March 1, 1984

Howard O'Connor's Tibetan Mastiff. Howard eventually grew to feel that this particular dog was irresponsibly aggressive. That is uncommon in this breed.

THE TOSA

The Tosa, sometimes known as the Japanese Fighting Dog or, in Japan, as the Tosa-Inu (Tosa Dog), is a breed which is little-known outside of Japan and is fairly rare even in its native land. It is also a breed which should have tremendous appeal to purebred dog enthusiasts, especially to those among us who are in search of an ideal family dog and an extremely effective man-stopping guardian.

Probably the best way to describe the Tosa to anyone who is unfamiliar with the breed would be to ask you to imagine a Mastiff reduced in size by about 30%. Now

Above: A close-up of Don Lee's "Mutsu" dog. *Opposite (top):* A proud Japanese owner with a very big dog. *Opposite (bottom):* A smiling, beguiling Tosa.

characteristics, and is probably more true to form now than it has ever been, is that these dogs are bred in Japan purely for functional purposes. While an occasional Japanese dog show does include a Tosa, these dogs are used primarily as arena fighters and often as guard dogs of the highest caliber. Few, if any, breeds have the initial hitting power of the Tosa. Probably no very large breed living today is as able to sustain prolonged combat as is the Tosa. Yet this breed is normally devoted to its human family and ready to defend its family and its home whenever it is called upon to do so. If the Tosa is extremely rare today (and it is), it is our mistake and misfortune, but fortunately it is a mistake which can easily be corrected.

The Tosa is a very quiet dog. Even when it is angry, it is angry in silence. This is due to the fact that one of the rules of the Japanese dogfight is that the Tosa must fight its battle in silence. Selective breeding of these dogs that comply to Japanese fighting rules has produced this characteristic of the Tosa. Some may feel that it is the dog's willingness to attack and dispatch a man that is important, not its method of threatening would-be intruders. The choice is yours. Personally, I prefer a quiet dog that I can rely upon to spring into action should the occasion to do so arise. Obviously, I am partial to the Tosa.

The Tosa has an interesting

imagine this 140- or 150-pound Mastiff without those negative physical characteristics that tell the observant purebred enthusiast all too clearly that the breed has lost its functional ability due to poor breeding practices. Finally, imagine that this Mastiff has the temperament of the mastiffs of England 600 years ago. Got it? This very large (but not gigantic), very athletic, and very determined mastiff-like dog is the Tosa.

The reason that the Tosa has retained its powerful physical and dominant temperamental

history but not an especially long one. It was during the latter half of the nineteenth century, when trade relations between the Eastern and Western worlds became firmly established, that Western dogs began being transported east and vice-versa. Dogfighting had been a long-standing tradition in Japan, as it had been throughout much of the world at that time, although the breeds which had been the traditional Japanese fighting dogs were of the lupoid (wolf-like) type as opposed to the molossoid (mastiff-like) type. Upon the arrival of many of the powerful Bulldog and Mastiff breeds of the West to Japan, it soon became obvious to Japanese dog fighters that, in order to produce a dog that would do well in the fighting arena against these Western breeds, Western component stock would have to be relied upon heavily. Soon Japanese dog fighters were blending the bloodlines of their traditional fighting dogs with bloodlines of the West in order to produce the ultimate combatant. Different breeders had different ideas about which Western dogs should be used in their breeding plans and in what proportions, thus, many different new lines were produced. The only real common denominator among them was that each was completely dominated by its Western breed admixture and clearly displayed this dominance in the appearance of

Donald Lee of Honolulu, Hawaii, with his terrific Tosa "Mutsu." Mutsu weighs 165 pounds and is shown in full ceremonial garb.

the line. The lines which were to become important to the development of the Tosa were the Tosa of the Mastiff line, the Tosa of the Bull Terrier line, the Tosa of the Great Dane line, the Tosa of the Bullmastiff line, and the Tosa of the Pointer line. Especially in the area in and around Kochi Prefecture of Shikoko Island, these fighting lines arose and the blending of these lines took place. All priorities were placed upon the functional abilities of the crossbred dogs, and, as a blended strain eventually began to reign supreme in the fighting arenas, only members of the crossbred type were bred to each other. Eventually a purebred type was developed.

Even after the purebred Tosa had been developed, the

emphasis of the breeding programs producing these dogs remained exclusively upon their functional value. This is evidenced by the fact that, during the 1930s, Japanese dog-fighting enthusiasts imported Bordeaux Dogue stock from France in order to cross this powerful fighting breed with Japan's Tosa dogs. This tells us that in Japan, as elsewhere, "purebred" is merely a modern descriptive term with no absolutely original functional value.

Today's Tosa dog is certainly a purebred by Western show standards and one which has retained its full functional value. Although the Japanese Kennel Club has established a written standard for the breed (and I have established the American standard for the breed), the Tosa remains primarily a fighter. Despite the common belief that the Akita is the largest of all Japanese breeds, the fact of the matter is that this distinction goes to the Tosa. While the average large male Tosa generally weighs between 140 and 150 pounds "chain weight" (the normal body weight of a dog on its chain) and about 115 pounds "pit weight" (the reduced weight of the dog in fighting condition), one Japanese Grand Champion stands at a chain weight of 198 pounds. This, however, is an unusually large functional Tosa. These weights are actual weights incidentally, and are not the kind of gross exaggeration so often offered by breeders of large show dogs.

Purebred enthusiasts interested in obtaining a Tosa are in luck. The breed is rare enough to have remained

These dogs are so athletic that it really makes you wonder why so many other giant breeds are not.

functionally valuable, yet it is not impossible to find these dogs. Many Tosas are owned by Hawaiian (as well as mainland) Tosa breeders, but unfortunately many of these are very poor representatives of the breed. Some, on the other hand, are excellent Tosas, and some Hawaiian breeders own terrific Grand Champion breeding stock. Tosas are beginning to spread elsewhere as well and, thus far, it seems that many breeders of these dogs are reputable and are breeding fine dogs.

As a guard dog with man-stopping ability, the Tosa is an excellent choice. The Tosa is a people-oriented dog that generally much prefers to be friends rather than enemies. It is a breed that becomes devoted to its human family, adults and children alike, and will get along well with guests to the house. It is, however, moderately suspicious of strangers, and will not hesitate to attack anyone who proves himself to be unworthy of its friendship. This is a very large and extremely powerful dog that is instinctively a fighter. It can wage a furious attack continuously for about fifteen or twenty minutes without becoming exhausted. As such, an attacking Tosa can hit a man with tremendous force and last through the battle that will ensue for a longer time than a man could endure under such

This Tosa was a big winner in the Japanese fighting arenas.

conditions. It has been selectively bred for many generations to endure the pain that is involved in a serious fight without running to escape. These are the qualities

Amazingly a large Tosa properly put together and weighing 130, 140 or even 150 pounds (or more!) can be nearly as agile as a Pit Bull.

that make the best guard dogs. Hopefully, purebred enthusiasts will fully discover this breed in the near future and strive to maintain its working abilities.

Standard for the Tosa (Japanese)

GENERAL APPEARANCE—Large-size dog with stately manner and robust build. The dog has hanging ears, short hair, square muzzle, dewlap, and hanging tail, thick root. The temperament is noteworthy for patience, composure, boldness, and courageousness.

SIZE—Minimum height 60½ centimeters for dogs, 54½ centimeters for bitches.

HEAD—The skull, broad; stop rather abrupt; the muzzle, moderately long. The nasal bridge, straight; and nose, large and black. The upper and lower jaws, strong; and teeth, strong with strong canine teeth and scissors bite.

Eyes—Slightly small and dark brown in color with expression of dignity.

Ears—Relatively small, rather thin, and set on high of skull sides, hanging close to cheeks.

NECK—Muscular with dewlap.

BODY—The withers, high, back, level and straight. The loins, broad muscular; croup, slightly arched at top. The chest, broad and deep; ribs, moderately sprung. The belly well drawn up.

TAIL—Set on high, thick at root, and tapering to the end, which reaches the hocks.

FOREQUARTERS AND HINDQUARTERS—The shoulders, moderately sloping. The forearms, straight, moderately long, and strong. The pasterns, slightly inclining and robust. Muscles of hind legs, very developed. The joints of stifle and hock, moderately angled and vigorous.

FEET—Tightly closed. The pads, thick and elastic. The nails, hard and dark in color (desirable).

GAIT—Robust and powerful.

COAT—Short, hard, and dense.

COLOR—Solid red is ideal, but white and red markings also permitted.

FAULTS—

Disqualifications—Monorchid or cryptorchid.

Major Faults—Shyness. Thin bone. Extremely overshot or undershot.

Minor Faults—Snipey muzzle. Slightly overshot or undershot.

Steve Ostuni with a great Tosa Dog being judged by Rick Tomita. Rick spotted the quality of this dog in a hurry and gave it Best in Show. Actually both Steve and I have handled this dog.

CONCLUSION

A feat surely impossible in a few months, Judy Hoover holds five Beaverbrook puppies. Rottweilers get to be big dogs.

In conclusion of this book on man-stopping guard dogs, I would like to emphasize a few points that I have already made throughout the course of it. I feel that this emphasis is necessary, as these points are of the utmost importance to anyone who owns or intends to own any of the dogs that we have discussed here.

As I have said repeatedly, it is my firm opinion that the primary motivation for obtaining a dog of any of the breeds discussed in this book should be very similar to the motivation that leads another person to obtain a friendly Golden Retriever for use as a family pet. Each of the breeds discussed is known to be an excellent companion in the proper environment.

Converting any good dog chosen from among the naturally dominant breeds from a would-be stable companion, family pet, and trustworthy home guardian into an overly aggressive and dangerous animal is generally a very easy matter. An untrustworthy personality is an easy thing to inflict upon any naturally "macho" dog, but it is not an easy thing to live with once it has been introduced. I have never known anyone who owned an overly aggressive dog of any breed who did not wish there was some way to ease the dog's temperament. Unfortunately, while cultivating a very aggressive temperament in a dog is a very simple matter, easing an aggressive temperament is a very difficult and often impossible task.

Simply because a guard dog does not make an obvious attempt to kill everyone it does not recognize by no means indicates that it is ineffective as a potential man-stopper. The most effective personal guard dogs are those that can be trusted to be kept at your side at all times. The least effective of all guards are those which are locked in the basement whenever a stranger arrives on the scene, due to the dog's inability to be trusted around people with whom it is not familiar. I will be the first to agree that the presence of a large dog is not sufficiently dependable as a serious deterrent against crime. A dog must be both physically

Assuming her place at the front door is WildWind's Mary, an American Staff pup owned by Chester and Lauraine Rodgers.

temperamentally suited to attack an intruder and make any further advance on the intruder's part impossible if it is to be considered an effective man-stopping guard dog. Of the two, I would feel more secure with a large but docile sheepdog in my home than with an overly aggressive guard dog. The ideal man-stopper is a combination of docility around friends and aggression toward intruders. As a dog is a trainable animal and not a defense machine, such a balance is very possible to achieve. Breeding alone can often provide this balance.

Some of the breeds of dog discussed in this book are very readily available, and it is an easy matter for the average person to obtain these dogs. Others among these are very rare and are not very easy to obtain. I would like to assure anyone who is in the market for one of these less-available dogs that persistence should eventually pay off, and that there is no breed discussed in this book that is impossible to obtain by anyone who is serious about finding it. One of the criteria that I used in including breeds in this book was the accessibility of puppies of each breed, and I personally located an available litter of well-bred puppies of each of these breeds before the book was written. At one point or another, I was offered a pup of each of the lesser known breeds, and, if I can locate these dogs, you can too. Do not let the seeming unavailability of any of these dogs deter you from owning one if you have chosen a

Two fawn Mastiff puppies at Winterwood Kennels. Photo by Ron Reagan.

particular breed based upon your research. Though some of these dogs are more expensive than others, all can be obtained if you are determined to own one.

Do not expect too much of a young dog too fast. Always bear in mind that a young puppy is an infant, just like any other infant, and, though it must be socialized and trained eventually, it must learn to act like a mature dog gradually and at its own pace. Particularly in the area of defense training, the learning process should not begin before the dog has reached sexual maturity and must proceed gradually once it has begun.

Some dogs are simply unsuitable as defense dogs. Even dogs born of the finest breeding among the boldest of breeds will sometimes be impossible to train for defense work. If you should happen to choose a puppy that never displays any ability as a capable defense dog upon maturity, forcing the issue will serve no useful purpose. Depending upon your personal situation and your needs, a decision will have to be made concerning your future with the animal, but any attempt to modify the very core of the dog's temperament will be a futile endeavor. Again, selecting your breed and your breeding wisely will absolutely minimize your chances of disappointment.

Be a friend to your dog and your dog will be a friend to you. Be aware of the fact that

your defense dog is essentially a living, breathing personality just like you are. In my opinion, making your dog's life an unhappy, unfulfilling one is as much of a travesty against nature as if your own life were being made unhappy by someone else. Above all, enjoy your pet's company and give it every opportunity to enjoy yours.

One day this tiny Tosa pup will grow up to stop a man as big as this one!

PIT BULL LIT: BOOKS WORTH KNOWING

The following books, published by T.F.H. Publications, Inc., represent an important component in the available literature about the American Pit Bull Terrier and his international (sometimes bigger) counterparts. These books are available directly from the publisher or at a local pet shop or bookstore.

The World of Fighting Dogs. By Carl Semencic, Ph.D.

H-1069. 287 pages. Color and Black/White photography. ISBN 0-86622-656-7

Dr. Semencic's first book revolving around the mastiff world, this controversial and unmistakably momentous volume has been raising eyes, hair and conversation since its first publication in 1981. It confronts the reader, ready or not, with a head-on discussion of dogfighting, providing accurate, frank details as well as a general background to the "sport." Among the fighting dogs included are the American Pit Bull Terrier, both Staffordshire breeds, Bull Terrier, Neapolitan Mastiff, Dogue de Bordeaux, Akita, Shar-Pei, Tosa and others. Acknowledging the controversial, illegal, and possibly illegitimate nature of the topic, Dr. Semencic presents his information in an intelligent, sensitive way which cannot help being rivetting reading.

THE WORLD OF RICHARD F. STRATTON

This is the American Pit Bull Terrier. *PS-613. Published 1976. 176 pages. Black/White photography. ISBN 0-87666-660-8.*
The Book of the American Pit Bull Terrier. *H-1024. Published 1981. 350 pages. Color and Black/White photography. ISBN 0-87666-734-5.*
The World of the American Pit Bull Terrier. *H-1063. Published 1983. 288 pages. Color and Black/White photography. ISBN 0-87666-851-1.*

Friend Stratton has written voraciously on his favorite breed, the American Pit Bull Terrier, without ever loosing his spark, heart or wit. These first three volumes have become standard "rep" for all persons interested and/or concerned about this most provocative, fearless canine. Important and historical dogs are illustrated in each book; many photos represent the only extant photo of a particular champion. While the approach and focal point of each book vary to degrees, all three volumes pour forth the author's wisdom, firsthand experience and unmitigated passion for the Pit Bull breed. Three musts.

The Truth About the American

Pit Bull Terrier. *TS-142. 320 pages. Over 300 full-color photos! ISBN 0-87666-638-9.*

Richard F. Stratton's fourth volume on the Pit Bull proves to be a most important addition to dog literature and the definitive edition to culminate his prior three prerequisite books. Published in 1991, *The Truth* reflects on the breed's very difficult past decade and validates the virtues of the dogs while discrediting the rumors which attempt to undo the Pit Bull. This book represents the breed fancy's insuppressible celebration; like the dogs themselves, this book is fearless, gripping and very powerful. Pit Bull fans and bullish antagonists alike will find this book difficult to put down.

RELATED DOG REFERENCE

Dogs and the Law. By Anmarie Barrie, Esq.
DS-130. 160 pages. 55 color illustrations. ISBN 0-86622-088-7

Better to know than be sorry! New Jersey lawyer offers a practical and reliable survey of laws pertaining to our dogs. Advices concerning liability, licenses, impoundment, vicious dogs, vehicles, insurance, wills, etc., etc. This book will prove valuable, enlightening, and even entertaining. Color drawings and cartoons illustrate the text.

The Atlas of Dog Breeds of the World. By Bonnie Wilcox, DVM, and Chris Walkowicz.
H-1091. 912 pages. 1,111 color photographs! ISBN 0-86622-930-2.

Traces the history and highlights the characteristics, appearance and function of every recognized dog breed in the world.

409 different breeds receive full-color treatment and individual study—over 35 mastiff breeds among the discussed. The authors treat the mastiff breeds individually and trace the group's common origins. This book is among the ultimate reference sources available in dog literature today.

The Mini-Atlas of Dog Breeds. By Andrew De Prisco and James B. Johnson.
H-1106. 576 pages, nearly 700 full-color photographs! ISBN 0-86622-091-7

An identification handbook giving a concise and thorough look at over 400 of the world's dog breeds. The authors' enthusiastic and knowledgeable approach brings to life instantly man's oldest friend and companion. A flowing and witty text, enlivened by nearly 700 photos, successfully maps out the world of dogs; an easy-reference format pinpoints each breed's development, portrait, registry, and pet attributes. The volume is captioned with specially designed symbols for information at the reader's fingertips.

The Staffordshire Terriers: American Staffordshire Terrier and Staffordshire Bull Terrier. By Anna Katherine Nicholas.
TS-143. 256 pages. 220 color photos; historical B/Ws. ISBN 0-86622-637-0.

Dog person and show judge for over 50 years, Nicholas offers concrete details about the foundation and development of the bull-and-terrier breeds. The author traces with professional precision the progress of the breeds in the conformation and obedience worlds in both the U.S. and England. Specifics on American, British, and Australian kennels for both breeds are included. For fanciers of these breeds and lovers of bull-and-terrier dogs, this book will prove indispensible for many years.

The Professional's Book of the Rottweiler
By Anna Katherine Nicholas. *TS-147. 432 pages. Approximately 600 full-color photos! ISBN 0-86622-625-7.*

Despite the critics' contention that Miss Nicholas's 1986 *The World of Rottweilers* would remain the definitive text on the breed for decades, this latest 1991 volume on the breed strengthens Nicholas's claim to fame in the Rottweiler world. *The Professional's Book of the Rottweiler* is the perfect companion to its predecessor volume, up-dating information and relaying new important data about the breed. For serious Rottweiler aficionados around the globe, this book will prove irreplaceable, truly resourceful, and nothing less than marvelous.

OTHER BREED BOOKS OF INTEREST
American Staffordshire Terriers. By Anna Katherine Nicholas. *KW-158. 192 pages. Over 175 color illustrations.*
The Boxer. By Anna Katherine Nicholas. *PS-813. 256 pages. 130 photographs. ISBN 0-86622-028-3.*
Bouviers des Flandres. By Gerene Coates Leggett. *KW-168. 192 pages. Over 175 color illustrations. ISBN 0-86622-691-5.*
Bullmastiffs. By Mary Prescott. *KW-163. 192 pages. Over 175 color illustrations. ISBN 0-86622-994-9.*

Bull Terriers. By Martin Weil. *KW-112. 192 pages. Over 175 color illustrations. ISBN 0-86622-715-9.*
The World of the Doberman Pinscher. By Anna Katherine Nicholas. *H-1082. 640 pages. 1,400 photos—800 in color! ISBN 0-86622-123-9.*
The Book of the Doberman Pinscher. By Joan McDonald Brearley. *H-968. 576 pages. Nearly 450 photos in color and B/W. ISBN 0-87666-658-6.*
The German Shepherd Dog. By Ernest H. Hart. *PS-810. 256 pages. 150 photos. ISBN 0-86622-031-3.*
The Book of the German Shepherd Dog. By Anna Katherine Nicholas. *H-1062. 480 pages. 480 photos. ISBN 0-87666-562-8.*
Giant Schnauzers. By Arthur S. Lockley. *KW-204. 192 pages. Over 175 color illustrations. ISBN 0-86622-574-9.*
The Great Dane. By Anna Katherine Nicholas. *PS-826. 320 pages. Over 100 color photos. ISBN 0-86622-122-0.*
Mastiffs. By Marie A. Moore. *KW-180. 192 pages. Over 175 color illustrations. ISBN 0-86622-687-7.*
The Book of the Rottweiler. By Anna Katherine Nicholas. *H-1035. 544 pages. Nearly 500 photos in color and B/W. ISBN 0-87666-735-3.*
The World of Rottweilers. By Anna Katherine Nicholas. *H-1083. 336 pages. 583 color photos; 79 B/W. ISBN 0-86622-124-7.*
The Rottweiler. By Richard F. Stratton. *PS-820. 256 pages. Over 100 photos. ISBN 0-86622-732-6.*

INDEX

Bold page numbers indicate breed chapters.